S0-AXR-418

THE ENGLISH SETTER

Mrs. Valerie Foss is a championship show judge of English Setters as well as other gundogs. She is the widow of Bill Foss who started the Elswood Kennel in 1943. There have been seven English Setter show champions bred or owned by the Foss's in English Setters. In this book is all the novice needs to know to enjoy owning an English Setter.

THE
ENGLISH
SETTER

VALERIE FOSS

FOYLES HANDBOOKS
LONDON

ISBN 0 7071 0579 X

© *W. & G. Foyle 1976*

First published 1976

Frontispiece by Anne Cumbers

Published in Great Britain by
W. & G. Foyle Ltd.,
125 Charing Cross Road,
London, WC2H 0EB

Printed and bound in Great Britain by
REDWOOD BURN LIMITED
Trowbridge & Esher

I dedicate this book to my late husband, Bill Foss, for it was through our marriage that I became involved in the world of English Setters. He was a most successful breeder and exhibitor and a well known judge but, the main thing, he never forgot, he, himself, had once been a novice. He is remembered in that absorbing world of dogs for his kindness for he was indeed Chaucer's 'perfect, gentle knight'. My thanks to Mr Goutorbe who wrote the chapter "on the qualifier" and especially to Mrs. D. Moon who deciphered my illegible handwriting. Not forgetting my friends who read through the chapters.

CONTENTS

LIST OF ILLUSTRATIONS

1

ORIGINS OF THE BREED

One of the oldest breeds of gundog, the English Setter's natural work has been described in literature since the Fourteenth Century. The Setters we know to-day were evolved over hundreds of years from Spaniels. Our first knowledge of Spaniels is from the work of the French Count Gaston de Foix who, in 1387, wrote his book called "Livre de Chasse". Early mention is made by Dr. Caius in his book published in 1570, dogs used in fowling — "by which was meant taking all manner of birds, and these dogs he divided into two kinds, those used on land and those that found game on the water". To the dog used with the net he gave the specific name of "Setter", two hundred years later the "Setting Spaniel" was still in use for the net and called by that name, while the term "Setter" was coming into general use for the dog employed in a similar manner with the gun. The Kennel Club Register for the breed was opened in 1873, but before this many aristocratic families preserved their own strains. Mr. Edward Laverack, born at Keswick in 1800, bought a pair of English Setters from the Rev. A. Harrison of Carlisle, about 1825, and from those two animals he built a strain — his animals were dual purpose. He died in 1877. Dog Shows were only first held in 1861 and Field Trials in public from 1866. Laverack had little opportunity to show what his dogs could do in both spheres before he died. Nevertheless, he made two champions and bred others for younger men to exhibit; the first of all gundog breeds to produce a Dual Champion (i.e. both field and bench) was the English Setter, the 100% Laverack Countess. It was Edward Laverack who drew up and published the standard of the English Setter in his book "The Setter" 1872. Mr. Edward

Purcell Llewellin founded his strain a few years later upon the Laverack's and, having owned numerous dual-purpose winners, he turned to working Setters only. Although Laverack and Llewellin aimed to produce their own individual ideal of English Setter each approached his goal in a different way. Laverack practised close inbreeding for generations within his own strain. Llewellin used a variety of other strains and individual dogs mixed with his own. In America working Setters called Llewellins since 1919 have had a separate register. In England the Kennel Club has never divided in separate registers the two distinct branches.

2

THE STANDARD
Reprinted by kind permission of the Kennel Club

he English Setter standard can be obtained from the
.ennel Club in the booklet entitled "Standards of the Breeds
– Sporting Breeds" and there, set out in writing, is the
erfect English Setter but, as one famous Gundog Judge has
aid, 'a standard is not an engineering blueprint'. Each
idividual interprets the standard in a slightly different way,
ast as words can have slightly different meanings. The
.nglish Setter standard is an old one, drawn up and first
ublished by Edward Laverack in "The Setter" in 1872 and
ememeber this standard was designed to give the perfect
ake and shape for a dog for work.

The English Setter Club was founded in 1890 and I have
ne of the original booklets of that year giving a list of
)fficials and Members, Rules, and the Description of the
.nglish Setter. That most famous of dog authors,
.tonehenge, in "The Dog" (in Health and Disease) 1859
ives the points of the English Setter in comparison with the
rish Setter and both compared against the Pointer. Nothing
urther was done standard wise until after the Setter and
•ointer Club was revived in 1936 and in its first Year Book
•ublished a standard of the English Setter taken from the
.nglish Setter Club. In 1948 the Kennel Club decided to
nake itself responsible for all breed standards and consulted
he clubs in each breed. The English Setter Club was
onsulted for that of English Setters, a slightly amended
ersion was taken by the Kennel Club as its version, and the
.ennel Club gave it the format of the Kennel Club Standard,
vhich came into force 1st January, 1950. The following is,
herefore, the standard with some explanatory notes of my
•wn.

THE ENGLISH SETTER

Characteristics — An intensely friendly and quiet nature dog with a keen game sense. These distinctive traits ar found in all English Setters, quietly loves his owner an adores children. Even the show bred Setter can still retai this keen game sense.

General Appearance — Of medium height, clean in outline elegant in appearance and movement. This section is bes described by the word balance, everything in proportion one flowing whole, no sharp angular lines. Graceful an refined. Now we go on to the separate parts of the dog and am reminded of an old adage 'one picture is worth a thousand words'. The first part is head and skull, an Baronet is lying on the floor near my desk. Still the sam beautiful head with the lovely true melting English Sette expression and he is now nearly 12 years old!

Head and Skull — Head should be long and reasonably lean with well defined stop. The skull oval from ear to ear showing plenty of brain room, and a well defined occipita protuberance. The muzzle moderately deep and fairl square; from the stop to the point of the nose should equa the length of skull from occiput to eyes; the nostrils wide and the jaws of nearly equal length; flews not to be too pendulous; the colour of the nose should be black or live according to the colour of the coat.

Ears — The ears of moderate length, set on low, and hangin in neat folds close to the cheek; the tip should be velvety, the upper part clothed in fine silky hair.

Mouth to be level.

This does indeed paint a word picture of the lovely head o the English Setter. Lean, with a well defined stop i.e. plenty of chiselling between the eyes, these to be reddish brown, the darker the better, the shape of the eye must not be too full o round. Egg shaped skull from ear to ear. Well defined bump on the back of the head. The muzzle, that part of the dog' head which is projected and contains the nose the mouth fairly deep and square. Not too much hanging lip or flew The ears set on about level with the eyes, neat and hanging close to the cheek, lovely velvety feel to the tip of the ear

THE STANDARD

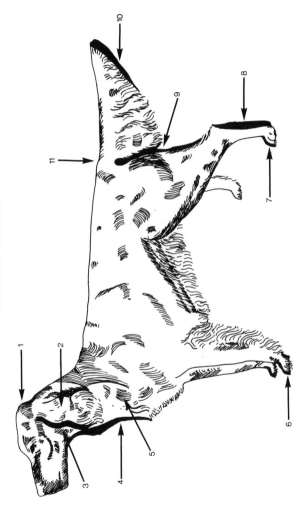

THE ENGLISH SETTER

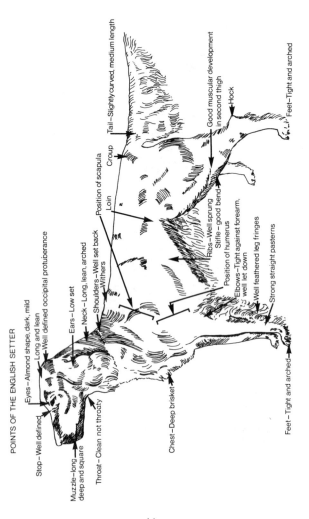

POINTS OF THE ENGLISH SETTER

Eyes – Almond shape, dark, mild

Long and lean

Well defined occipital protuberance

Stop – Well defined

Ears – Low set

Neck – Long, lean, arched

Muzzle – long deep and square

Throat – Clean not throaty

Shoulders – Well set back

Withers

Position of scapula

Loin

Croup

Tail – Slightly curved, medium length

Good muscular development in second thigh

Hock

Feet – Tight and arched

Ribs – Well sprung

Stifle – good bend

Position of humerus

Elbows – Tight against forearm, well let down

Well feathered leg fringes

Strong straight pasterns

Chest – Deep brisket

Feet – Tight and arched

14

higher up the ear covered in fine silky hair.

Mouth — Although the Setter is not a retrieving breed a good mouth is essential. The standard says mouth to be level which means top and bottom teeth should meet exactly, however, also accepted as correct for the Setter is the scissor bite, in which the top front teeth touch and slightly overlap the bottom.

The Neck — Neck should be rather long, muscular and lean, slightly arched at the crest, and clean cut where it joins the head; towards the shoulder it should be larger and very muscular, not throaty or pendulous below the throat, but elegant in appearance.

Once again that telling word elegant — the English Setter's neck should be like that of a thoroughbred horse. The neck is very closely allied to the formation of the shoulders. For perfection, the neck and shoulders must together be perfect, any fault will disturb the symmetry. Necks and Shoulders, like horse and carriage, run together. One often sees a bad neck fitted into equally bad shoulders, but only rarely does one find a bad neck set into good shoulders. Of course, the trouble is we have to decide what makes a good or bad neck. The words "rather long" in the standard are vague, like R. H. Smythe, M.R.C.V.S., the famous canine author says "the Giraffe necked ladies of Africa measure their own standard of beauty by the number of metal rings piled on top of the other, they can wear around their necks". Many judges feel the same way about dogs and write that certain dogs scored over other dogs in greater reach of neck, still the ability to wear half a dozen collars is not the criterion. The important thing is every part of the dog must be in perspective, it must all balance. The neck carries and supports the head so in proportion of size and weight they must match. Just as the crest of the neck should be slightly arched and the head fit neatly, so should the lower end of the neck merge into the withers and shoulders. It should not be easy to say where the neck finishes and the body starts.

Forequarters — The shoulders should be well set back or

oblique; the chest should be deep in the brisket, and of good depth and width between the shoulder blades. The forearm big and very muscular, with rounded bone, and the elbow well let down. Pasterns short, muscular, round and straight.

To imagine the correct forequarters, strip the dog of flesh mentally and see only the skeleton, thus a sloping scapula. For a Setter the angle between the mid-line of the scapula and the shaft of the humerus will approximate a right angle of 80° and that will show a correct lay back of shoulder. Deep chest, and width between the shoulder blades, which you can test with your sense of touch. Rounded bone self-explanatory. The position of the elbow joint takes up to the chest wall depends upon the length of the humerus and the angle it forms with the scapula at the shoulder joint. Also the muscle formation can have a great deal to do with whether the elbows stand off from the body. Also any bowleggedness will force the elbows out. Pasterns, part of the leg which 'flows' into the feet, to be short, muscular, round and straight.

Body — The body should be of moderate length, the back short and level with good, round, widely sprung ribs and deep in the back ribs, that is, well ribbed up. Again we must think of balance, moderate length — avoiding extremes, the back short and level, that is, a horizontal line, round widely sprung ribs, well ribbed up.

Hindquarters — The loins should be wide, slightly arched, strong and muscular, with defined second thigh. Stifles well bent and rugged, thighs long from hip to hock.

The loin is the part of the dog overlying the lumbar vertebrae. The second thigh is the part of the limb extending from the stifle to the hock. Well bent stifles. Good reach of thigh from hip to the point of the hock.

Feet — The feet should be very close and compact, and well protected by hair between the toes.

In feet there are several different kinds — the difference is the ability to bring the toes together in a bunch which gives us the cat foot of the English Setter.

Tail — The tail should be set on almost in line with the back,

16

medium length, not curly or ropy, to be slightly curved or scimitar-shaped, but with no tendency to turn upwards; the flag or feather hanging in long pendant flakes. The feather should not commence at the root, but slightly below, and increase in length to the middle, then gradually taper off towards the end; the hair long, bright, soft and silky, wavy, but not curly.

Judges usually measure the tail to the point of hock, for length, and it must not go past that.

Coat — The coat, from the back of the head in a line with the ears, ought to be slightly wavy, long and silky, which should be the case with the coat generally. The breeches and forelegs, nearly down to the feet, should be well feathered.

Colour — The colour may be either black/white (blue-belton), lemon/white (lemon-belton), liver/white (quite rare), black, white and tan, that is, tricolour; those without heavy patches of colour on the body, but flecked all over, preferred.

Weight and Size — Should be: Dogs — 60-66 lbs., height: 25½" — 27".

Bitches — 56-62 lbs., height 24" — 25½".

Faults — Coarse, lumpy shoulders, short foreface, tapering to nose, lack of 'stop', light or obliquely set eyes, high ear placement, loose elbows from bad shoulder placement, flat ribs, too long loin, wide feet, weak pasterns, straight stifles, narrow quarters, gay 'flag', lightness of bone, mouth undershot or overshot, lacking freedom of action.

Note: Male animals should have two apparently normal testicles fully descended into the scrotum.

3

CHOOSING A PUPPY

So you have gone into the pro's and con's of owning a dog and decided the English Setter is the one for you. With his mild gentle nature, his ability to tolerate and love all children, and his all round family appeal you have chosen the English Setter. Well a few things to remember, he is a gundog so requires adequate exercise, his attractive coat casts so from the beginning do not let that beguiling puppy get on to the furniture. Not everybody wants to leave your home in a hair suit! Even if you never show him, certain areas must be trimmed to keep him neat, that is, trimmed feet bring less mud into the kitchen than untrimmed ones. I know from experience, although the salesman who once asked "what sort of vinolay I had in mind" thought I was mad when I answered "muddy brown with black paw marks". He has an iron will under that velvet appeal and must be taught his basic obedience early on.

Where to get that puppy from? Write to the Kennel Club, 1 Clarges Street, Piccadilly, LONDON, W1Y 8AB, and ask for the names and addresses of some breeders or the name and address of the Secretary of the breed clubs. Write or telephone a breeder in your locality and tell him exactly what you want. If you think you might want to show tell the breeder — not all the puppies in the litter will be show standard, also the price of the puppies will vary slightly for what purpose they are wanted. Let us suppose you want your puppy as a pet and the breeder lets you choose your own puppy, arrange in plenty of time when you will call. Puppies, after they are fed, tend to go asleep so go before feeding time. The puppy you choose should be sturdy — no distended tummy, just roundly plump, bright eyes, clear skin, and should be alert and friendly. If they all seem to fulfil these conditions your choice will probably be swayed by some particular marking on the puppy's coat. Choosing the best puppy from a litter is not easy even for an expert, but an experienced breeder who knows their line has a better chance of success. To choose the best from a litter is one of the most fascinating areas of dog breeding, but choosing the best at 8/12 weeks is always a gamble.

If you want your puppy for show and breeding go to a kennel known for producing and selling winning stock. How do you find out where to meet some breeders? Order from your local newsagent one of the weekly dog papers — "Our Dogs" or "Dog World", in both are listed future shows. Go to some of the championship and big open shows and talk to the breeder whose stock you most admire. Most breeders really do want to help and if they, themselves, have nothing will put you on to somebody who has something suitable. Now choosing the puppy for show, watch them running about and then examine them individually on a table. Remember, the colour on an 8/12 weeks English Setter is not stabilised yet. Usually, the flecking is lighter than it will be as an adult. Patches are, of course, the same all the time — remember, the standard says "lightly flecked all over preferred". The dark eye patch can add a little extra winsomeness and many famous Sh. Ch's. have had eye patches. The puppy should be well reared with good bone and sturdy limbs, and the head in balance with the rest of the puppy. The muzzle should be square and not cut off short, the skull oval from ear to ear, the ears set on low (level with the eyes) long enough to reach the tip of the nose, 'work' between the eyes, that is, indentation, not level, dark eyes. Good pigmentation which means black nose, except in the case of a lemon belton when flesh coloured nose is allowed, black eye rims — if only a spot of pink on the eyerims this should disappear by the time the puppy is 6 months. Check the mouth — if the puppy's mouth has uneven teeth or an undershot jaw (the top teeth falling well behind the bottom ones), this should not right itself. Correct bite is a level scissor, top teeth slightly overlapping and touching the bottom teeth. Straight front legs, tight, small rounded feet, front legs not too close together, elbows well tucked in.

Now on to the neck and shoulders — shoulders laid well back, shoulders that are straight tend to go with not enough neck. The amount of neck that makes even the puppy look balanced, middle piece of the puppy short coupled, deep chest. The hindquarters — good bend of stifle, hocks turning neither in nor out, tail carrying on the topline of the puppy. Temperament again that happy bouncy puppy.

When you leave with your puppy you should have the pedigree form, the registration card to show it is registered with the Kennel Club, and a transfer form signed by the breeder ready for you to transfer into your name with the Kennel Club; from January 1975 the transfer fee is £1.00. If the breeder has not registered the puppies you can send to the Kennel Club for a form for registration by any other person than the breeder, cost £2.00. If you really want to breed several litters and show your animals you will probably wish to take out your own kennel name or suffix, such as my own of ELSWOOD. It appears before or after the dog's name e.g. Sh.Ch. *ELSWOOD* Highlight or Evening Flight of *Frejendor*. The Kennel Club has a new ruling which says that the kennel name must appear as a prefix i.e. before the name if the dog is bred by the owner, and a suffix i.e. after the name if bred by a person other than the owner.

Sh. Ch. Elswood Renmark Baronet

Sh. Ch. Suntop Royalbird

Sh. Ch. Iroquois Strathspey

Sh. Ch. Elswood Renmark Baronet and Sh. Ch. Ernford Chaffinch

Sh. Ch. Fenman Fragrance and Sh. Ch. Engsett Electrode

Sh. Ch. Elwsood Ashpenda Moonquest and Sh. Ch. Bournehouse Meadowfern

Sh. Ch. Trodgers Meadow Fescue and Sh. Ch. Yankee of Neighbours

Sh. Ch. Ednasid Merrell Blue Baron

4

ADULT FEEDING

Whatever purpose you have bought your puppy for — show, work, a companion or a combination of all three, you will want a strong, healthy dog and this you will only get with correct feeding. Just as balance makes the best specimen lookwise, balance is the word to remember in feeding. Nothing out of proportion. In the chapter on puppies you will find a diet sheet for your puppy. When you get your puppy from the breeder, you should get a diet sheet showing exactly how he has been fed, continue with this at least for the time being. If you want to change any sort of food do so gradually. A change of food too quickly can upset your puppy. There are many different methods of feeding dogs, but basically they fall into three categories.

Natural Rearing — in which the food is fed raw and as many natural foods are used. Meat is fed raw. Meat and biscuit meal are never given together. As well as wholemeal biscuit meal other cereals are used, barley and oat flakes. In addition, vegetables and herbs.

Orthodox Methods — Cooked meat cut up and mixed with biscuit meal which has been previously soaked with meat or vegetable juice.

Complete Foods — This third method seems to arouse the most heat in discussions on feeding. Basically, I feel it is a method designed for the convenience of the person looking after the dogs. The name 'complete foods' describes it perfectly, usually in pellet form it contains protein, cereal, bone meal, trace elements plus Vitamins, and its advocates would say that it is very much a complete food, that is, nutritionally balanced it is usually fed dry and plenty of water must be available for the dogs at all times. There are many brand names on the market — Purina, Vitalin, Solo, Maintain, etc. I, personally, have never used complete foods as a complete method of feeding, always on conventional foods, but my dogs after their morning milk have a breakfast of Purina.

Growing puppies need vitamins and certain minerals (see Puppy Feeding Chapter). As long as his diet is well balanced the adult dog needs few additions; Vivonium made by Crookes is excellent. The exceptions are stud dogs and bitches in whelp. The adult dog should be fed twice a day; a breakfast of milk then a few biscuits or a small bowl of complete food, main meal late afternoon. Average amount of food for an adult English Setter 1½-2 lbs. dry weight but, of course, it varies with individual dogs. The dog's condition is the best guideline.

INOCULATION

Consult your veterinary surgeon for when he likes to inoculate. This can be done at 8 weeks, but many wait till 12/13 weeks. Obviously, you will tend to use the vaccine your vet recommends, but those that inoculate against Hard Pad, Distemper and Hepatitis, and the two forms of Liptospirosis really everything are recommended. I, myself, use Canilep. Until your puppy has been inoculated do not take him out on the roads nor mix with other dogs.

"FADDY FEEDERS"

A thin dog which defies all efforts to put on flesh, especially if you are showing him, can be a heartache. Check with your veterinary surgeon that it is not something physically wrong with the dog — internal parasites, etc. Worms can cause certain mineral deficiencies and stop normal growth. Sometimes the environment, bitches in season, too close confinement, lack of exercise, is the fault. If the dog eats well, but does not put on weight change the time of feeding, divide the food into smaller portions, feed three times daily, plenty of carbohydrate (milk is a good fattener), suet, porridge, herrings (tinned or fresh), all may be included in a thin dog's diet. There are nowadays, on the market, special foods developed as a weight gaining plan. Although many dogs eat better in the company of others, the faddy feeder is often better fed alone. English Setters are not greedy dogs and need to eat all that is given them.

5

KENNELS

The ideal home for the English Setter is in the house. One or
two dogs can be kept comfortably in this way but, of course,
once you get beyond this number this plan is no longer the
ideal. Remember that the housing of dogs is one of the most
important features of kennel management and the part it
plays in maintaining the dog in perfect health must never be
underrated. There are three things which will stop your dog
being in good condition, these being dirt, damp and
draughty kennels. There are many different kennels on the
market and I would advise a thorough investigation of each
type and what you think you need. Before buying or building
your kennels plan carefully and take everything into
consideration. As near to the house as possible, large enough
for puppy rearing and whelping, a section for storage of
bedding and dry food, and if you are converting brick
buildings already there, with facilities for cooking and
refrigerator, the ultimate ideal a kennel kitchen. You can buy
wooden kennels. Nowadays there are steel kennels on the
market specially treated so that they do not rust. You can
also build your own from concrete blocks. Inside a bunk or
box for sleeping. The bed should measure at least 5' x 4' for
two dogs. The best bedding wheat straw or wood wool and
sawdust on the floor. Garden sheds can be converted into
kennels provided they have windows so they are really
draught proof line with hardboard. Any kennel must have
good ventilation, it should be high up so that any incoming
air is well above the level of the dogs. These kennels can be in
a run of either cement, slabs, brick, grass or cinders,
remembering that drainage is an important factor. Grass can
become far too muddy in wet weather and dogs tend to run

...wyn English Setters ready for
 walk

Colour photos by Anne Cumbers

Three Suntop English Setters

Silverteal puppies

An inquisitive Silverteal
puppy

Large bone for teeth and play

Ch. Suntop Winter Breeze

Fine Litter of Suntop English Setters in a puppy run

A little comfort in old age

up and down the same routes which does not help. Cinders get very dusty in hot weather. Cement or slabs are probably the best in my opinion, and have duck boards for the dogs to lie on. Chain link around the run buried 6″ in the ground or cemented in, at least 6′ in height. Gates opening inwards with the bolt that can be manipulated from inside or outside. Let the runs be as large as possible.

Never put wet dogs away without drying them well, especially the feathering. Use a wash-leather and lukewarm water or thick towelling. If your dogs are anything like mine they will end up rushing round with the towel! Cleanliness is the main rule with the kennels. All excreta removed from kennels and run each morning. Clean water down all the time. English Setters are foot paddlers I have found, and a wedged bucket seems to be the best. In the summer months kennel work becomes much easier because the dogs will lie out in the sun, but in the short days of winter and especially in bad weather, you must remember you cannot leave dogs shut in their kennels for hours and expect them to be clean. Exercise which I consider not only essential, but one of the best aspects of owning a dog, and by exercise I mean organised exercise. This does not enter into the life of young puppies, which get all they need playing together, but the six months old puppy must start with regular lead exercise every day see that adults have a certain amount of road walking, and then free-running in a safe place. If dogs are not exercised regularly they have poor muscular development, not only of the muscles of the skeleton, but also of important internal muscles.

HOUSE TRAINING A PUPPY

Do not expect your puppy to be trained within a week. One thing which is always a great help puppies relieve themselves after eating. You cannot expect your puppy to be clean until at about five months it may start to 'last' through the night. Always take the puppy to the same place in the garden or yard. After feeding always take the puppy out, when it wakes from sleep through the day, first thing in the morning, last thing at night and in between times. Give great praise when the puppy does what is correct. Never rub the puppy's nose in any mistakes, but let the puppy see it has done wrong by the tone of your voice and take it outside at once.

6

TRAINING AND SHOW TRAINING OF YOUR ENGLISH SETTER

When you bring your puppy home from his breeder he must learn to sleep on his own. He is used to cuddling up to his brothers and sisters and that first night will probably cry. See that he has a box big enough for him to lie in comfortably and some warm, soft bedding, some newspaper in front for mistakes, and the rest of the room partitioned off so that he has not got too large an area which, in the dark, he could get lost. When ready to put him to bed give him his last meal or drink, take him to the place where you want him to relieve himself, then put him to bed. I find a large marrow bone keeps the puppy occupied. Turn out the light and no matter how heartrending the cries seem do not weaken, but leave the puppy till morning. Puppies play hard and then drop off to sleep so quickly; these sleep times are important, so if you have children do not let them bother the puppy when he wants to sleep. Actually, during the time he sleeps in the day, it is ideal to put him in the place where you wish him to sleep. The ideal is two puppies, as they play and occupy each other! In house training it is better to prevent the mistake.

Before you take your puppy on the road get him used to a collar and lead in the house or garden. At first he will try to scratch it off, but will soon get used to it. At first choose quiet roads so the traffic is gradually got used to? From when you first let your puppy off the lead in a safe place, see that when you call he comes back at once, reward him and remember this basic piece of obedience is the most important thing you will ever teach him. Most English Setters love cars. Take him a short journey at first. If you find on long journeys he is sick give him a canine travel sickness pill. See that he learns to stay in the car without you. My dogs love the car and if they are in the yard and the car door is open will all climb in and go to sleep.

If you want to show your Setter a few visits to shows to watch them being handled is worth pages of instructions. The mirror used in trimming is ideal for setting up your dog and seeing how he looks, if you have nobody to help you. Many clubs have handling classes and these are a great help in getting your puppy used to other dogs in a confined space. In the show-ring you are expected to show your dog to its best advantage. This means moving him in the way the judge wants, at the right pace, and without him pulling either to the front or side. Standing him with the front legs straight, not too far forward, nor too far back, the hindlegs slightly spread apart and slightly back to give the required level topline. Hand under dog's chin, holding head up and stretching the neck out, but be careful not to hold his head too high. With the other hand, hold either middle or tip of tail very lightly in a straight line with the back. Plenty of praise and practise the standing each day. Remember, if you try to force the dog to stand in an unnatural stance he will start to move, so relax and let him 'set up' in a relaxed fashion. Only experience will make you a good Setter handler, but watch the best — they know exactly when to let their dogs relax, when to get their attention, when to praise and when they, themselves, should stop chatting to the exhibitor standing next to them. If your puppy has not been registered with the Kennel Club he must be before you can show him, so write to The Secretary, The Kennel Club, 1 Clarges Street, Piccadilly, LONDON, W.1., for a form for registration by any other person than the breeder. Cost of registration this way is £2.00 and remember to get the breeder to sign this form.

A dog tends to cast his coat once a year, a bitch more often — the quicker the dead coat is combed out the quicker the new coat will come through. An English Setter being shown out of coat is at a great disadvantage so do not be tempted.

7

THE QUALIFIER

For this chapter on the Qualifier I would like to thank Mr Réne Goutorbe of the Upperwood English Setters who so ably wrote it. He has what is needed for such a chapter, practical experience.

Nothing is more attractive than the sight of a pointing dog at work on heather, stubble or any open field. We are fortunate today to have some reasonable workers among our show English Setters. It would be wrong to think that because you own an English Setter, you have a dog who one day is going to win top awards at field trials. This is not so since most breeders of show English Setters concentrated their thoughts on type and conformation and hardly considered the working abilities of the dogs they bred from. On the other hand, the great breeders of working English Setters bred from the best working stocks without paying much attention to the type... These two different approaches led to the actual situation where we have two totally separate breeds of English Setters: The Show English Setter whose standard should be as close as possible to that described by Edward Laverack, and the working English Setter, sometimes called "Llewellen" whose standard very often tends to be rather distant from that established by Laverack but whose working abilities are in many cases exceptional. The aim of the qualifier is not to reach with a dog the standard of work of a field trial champion, but to demonstrate in front of two field trial judges that the candidate is worthy of his title of Champion when he gains his 3rd Challenge certificate at a Championship Show. In order to be eligible to take a qualifying certificate a setter or a pointer must have been awarded one Challenge certificate.

The owner of a Challenge certificate winner should have no great difficulty in qualifying his dog if the latter shows himself a keen natural worker with game sense. The day he takes his qualifier the setter will have to display his working abilities by quartering the ground, finding game, pointing and being steady to the gun. As the setter has to find game, a certain amount of luck is involved as it may happen that the dog will have to run on a ground deserted by birds. However a dog who quarters the ground thoroughly has a better chance to find game and deserves more praise than the potterer who eventually might bump into a bird.

THE TRAINING

Let us assume that the candidate to a qualifier is a dog who is used to free galloping not only on the back lane, but in open fields, that he has already met game, perhaps the odd pheasant or game, that he has shown his interest by chasing them!!.... He must now realise that chasing hare or partridge will not lead him anywhere. He must hunt, of course but not for himself, but for his handler, eventually for the guns for whom he will have to find game.

Some initial training can be performed in the back garden. However there is always the possibility of being disturbed. Personally I prefer to train my dogs in the right environment. Moreover having grouse moorlands in the vicinity of my kennels, this helps matters. I know that in some areas it is becoming more and more difficult to obtain training ground but generally speaking, I think that the prospective trainer, particularly if known locally for having his dogs properly under control, with the right approach to farmers or game keepers can usually get some land to run his dogs. One must not be too dogmatic regarding the training. The methods obviously vary from one trainer to another, moreover setters and pointers having their own individuality, the way of training one dog might be totally different to that used or another. This is what makes training so fascinating. The art of it is to fine point the weaknesses of one dog and endeavour to correct them, at the same time the natural qualities of the pupil must be cultivated. Before starting the training in the field, it is essential that a close relationship should be created between the handler and the dog. It is no use trying to prepare a setter for a qualifier if he does not trust his trainer. Once this relationship exists the initial training can be started. Now armed with one or two whistles, a check card and lots of energy, one can start the training sessions which should be short and enjoyable for the dog and the handler. It is impractical training your dog if after most sessions you are going to feel depressed and frustrated by the bad performance of your pupil and his lack of progress. If you feel certain that although your dog is a potential worker, but at one stage he does not seem to make any progress under your training let him have a rest, leave him in his kennel, he is certainly confused, perhaps he has learnt too much too soon, only take him on walks on the lead, and you will be surprised to see, when you re-commence the training that his rest has been worthwhile. Your dog will show keenness again, and in my opinion, it is always easier to stop a dog who goes rather than trying to make one go.

When I train a dog for work or for that matter for the qualifier, I never let him have any galloping with my other setters or pointers as I find that my pupil is then inclined to take bad habits, and precious hours of training can be wasted this way. If I find that my dog or myself are not in the right frame of mind to undertake any training one day, I either leave the dog to run in the paddock or merely take him on the lead along the lane. The setter must always look forward to all his training sessions. Some dogs have a better natural ability to quarter than others. Some setters who have not enough confidence or lack experience tend to stay in the trainers way and seem not to dare quartering. It would be wrong to dismiss these dogs as hopeless, and although very often the beginning might be very difficult indeed and frustrating, what a feeling of satisfaction goes through you the day your dog starts quartering.

In many cases those slow starters become very good workers. Different methods can be used to get a good quartering from your setter. First let us take the dog who goes, but is perhaps over keen whose quartering is rather erratic, hence somewhat hard to control: The check cord will be the vital instrument used to master the pupil. This cord will consist of about 30 metres of nylon line. The cord can either be looped around the dog's neck or attached to its collar. When the dog is either control to the right or to the left, let the rope run loosely behind him, as soon as you require him to turn in, blow your turning whistle and use your turning hand signal. There is a great chance that any of these turning calls will not be observed. This is the moment to tread swiftly on the cord and blow the turning whistle at the same time. The check cord can also be operated with your hand which should be protected by a leather glove. When the dog has turned he must be encouraged with kind words to go in the other direction, the trainer must then run a short distance in front of him. Eventually the dog should overtake the trainer. He should be praised again, and when required to turn in the turning whistle and hand signal must be used with the check cord if necessary. Some setters and pointers are quicker to learn than others, nevertheless if your dog is bright and keen, it should not be long before he reaches an adequate standard of quartering. It is very important that this operation be carried out up wind. The less enthusiastic candidate to a qualifier will need a very fit handler, often prepared to run as much, if not more than his trainee, especially at the early stages of the training. The methods used will vary from one particular trainer to another, the sort of training ground also plays an important part. I always take my fast overkeen young working English Setters on tall heather in order to slow them down to ensure a better control over them. On the other hand, if a setter, perhaps because it has never met any game yet, and is still in a state of confusion, potters around and does not show any positive quartering, one should be wise to take him on easy ground, and if possible with plenty of game, this in order to kindle the fire in him. My pointer bitch, Northwood-Yrette has always been of great assistance to me in the training of

ppies. If you have the probability of approaching a setter
 pointer man, owner of a reasonable working dog, you
uld ask him to have a few runs with him. His dog does not
ve to be a field trial champion! the quartering does not
ve to be perfect! Perhaps at first, the novice will follow his
ore experienced companion, but the day will soon come
en your setter will take some initiative. The companion
ght come to point. You should not worry if your setter
als his companion's point, flushes the birds and even
ases: calmly get your dog back, this might not be easy, put
n on the lead and pat him. Oh Yes, pat him and praise him,
ur setter is not a potterer any more and my word, he can
, perhaps too much, but never mind, you are now full of
thusiasm and I am sure quite fit. Now it is time to let your
g have a few days rest at home and to prepare yourself for
ore advanced training. I must confess that you will
rtainly need patience, toughness blended with kindness for
ur future "full Champion". A few fellow trainers will
rtainly agree with me, but I think that one must try to
velop as much as possible the natural instinct of the setter,
d only when he reaches a reasonable standard of
artering, emphasis should be exercised on obedience. If
e dog quarters well as long as he has a good nose, half the
ttle is won and you can look forward to handling him the
y he takes his qualifier. Obviously he must not be gun shy,
t steadiness to the gun, the way he keeps on point will
ten depend on your future training and handling. As our
g is now a reasonable quarterer, turns quite well to the
istle and hand command, we must be able to drop him
enever it is necessary. If this part of the training has not
en started yet, it should be introduced at this stage when
e setter is really keen and eager to get on with his work. If
e dog is still lacking in confidence and is still very erratic, it
advisable to postpone for a few weeks this exercise which
this case will only confuse him and slow him down. But let
 concentrate on this keen quarterer who is now ready to
ach a more advanced part of his training. The moment he
ould be taught to drop is when he passes in front of the

handler, quartering either from left to right or vice-versa
handler should then move swiftly forward to face the d
wave his right hand and give a command by using voice a
whistle. Each individual handler adapts his own word
command. It should be stressed that the words used mus
the same all the time. You must vary the tone of your voic
express to your dog your feelings concerning his work a
progress, do not make a speech to your dog, the vocabul
used should be as limited as possible. Obviously any sette
pointer is not going to drop the first time the trainer blo
his whistle or raises his hand, but as man faces the dog,
can easily interrupt his quartering and by holding his n
and applying his left hand on his back can readily put hin
a sitting position. The handler should then praise the pu
and keep on repeating the drop command, us
alternatively the voice and the whistle, with his hand rais
After a while he will even be able to walk backwards, a sh
distance away from the dog, staring at him and if necess
using the command again if he feels the dog intends to get
After putting the dog on the lead he must be praised and c
off again. This exercise should not be repeated too ofter
your pupil might lose interest. In due course the dog sho
be dropped at a small distance away from the handler a
after more training sessions further away. But a dog is no
machine and do not be surprised if after days and days
training, when you think your dog is under your compl
control, you try to drop him, on this occasion he seems to
entirely deaf, he does not hear your whistle and
disappears on the other side of the hill. Do not panic and
not run after him and above all do not chastise him when
comes back. Your dog has probably scented game... U
your check cord next time you go out. Now our dog quart
quite well, turns to the whistle, drops to the command, n
too bad, is it? Well, he was deaf last time we took him c
but never mind. Perhaps he chased a hare. That's naugh
Nevertheless, according to the rules this will not disqua
him. However, it is not quite correct, we must cure h
because he could be inclined to be a hare chaser, and if y

ry to qualify him on the Scottish moors, he could be spending his time running after the numerous blue hares and cooling off in the burns. This has been seen and I do not think that the judges who had to cope with large stakes were very amused by this type of demonstration for a qualifier.

Our dog may have an inclination to run into birds and chase them, or else to point them and run after them once they are flushed. It is hoped that the dog who has a tendency not to set (this term is used for setters) or point (term applied to pointers) will eventually do the job he is required to perform... Some handlers think that the best dogs are those who do not point at an early stage in life... Our concern is to have a dog who is fully trained to take his qualifier, and for that test he will have to point and show steadiness to the gun. This part of the training will have to take place with wild birds. Some trainers, I am told, are successful in using domesticated pheasants or quails or even pigeons. They are placed in cages in the field, under some leaves or straw. I tried this method, unfortunately my dogs have never shown very much interest in captive birds, it is certainly worth trying, if successful, this method would undoubtedly save time to anybody who has not any game within a short distance from his house. The conditions required for running the dogs would be ideal if one could choose a not too dry or cold day with a moderate breeze. The perfect training ground should be sufficiently covered, thus allowing enough birds to be found in order to give the dogs a good chance by having one or two points to encourage him. To gain his qualifier a dog should acknowledge game by pointing: when approaching birds he should at this stage slow down and gradually freeze with the nose pointed in the direction of the birds. To be exact, when the setter is in this immobile and crouching position, he is setting. The day he takes his qualfiier, if after giving a good quartering demonstration a setter has a point, he should not be far off his final success. It will now depend very much on the skill in handling the dog. Many young dogs at this stage will be excited and will easily chase as soon as a bird rises up. This is the reason why for this delicate part of the training, the handler must be decisive and act in a most careful manner. By now the handler will have spent several weeks walking up wind with his dog, and even if his pupil is not entirely under proper control yet, a certain partnership should exist between man and dog. Therefore the handler should be apt to decide how to master this critical moment he will have to come up against for the qualifier. It is quite often possible for the handler to notice when his dog has the scent of birds. When this occurs particularly with a young and eager setter, the safest move is to drop him and slip the check cord around his neck, to pat him and give a few words of praise. Let us hope that when he is moved forward, the birds will not be too wild and will sit tightly. If the dog is too eager to go, he should be firmly held by the check cord, some quiet words, such as "steady" should be whispered to him. As he moves nearer to the game, he will either get more excited or freeze. In the former case he should be stopped sharply with the check cord and held firmly in a still position. When he has calmed down, he should be held short on the lead or by the collar, this will certainly give more control over him. It is now known that the bird is not far in front of him and is going to rise any moment. For this occasion the dog will have to be shot over. Perhaps it will be the first time a shot has been fired near him. Even a dog of a very good disposition could easily be disturbed by a bang near his head, consequently if the handler has not the assistance of anybody firing the gun a few yards away, he should fire an ordinary starting pistol kept inside his pocket (an anorak with a padded pocket to smother the bang is ideal for this purpose). Now the setter is acknowledging the presence of the bird, obviously the experienced one should be on point without being told by his handler. As he has been in this immobile position for one or two minutes, he should now be led forward, slowly, with quiet praising words so as to make him understand that he has to be very careful, then the expected moment arrives. The bird is flushed, the shot is fired, perhaps our overkeen dog will try to rush forward to chase the game, but he will be

ld back firmly by his handler and commanded to stay still
r one or two minutes. This exercise repeated a dozen times
d our novice dog can then be promoted. He can be
leased from his check cord... Our candidate to a qualifying
rtificate can now quarter, his nose is good enough to find
rds and point, he is steady to the gun, although steadiness
not absolutely essential for a qualifying certificate. We
ow, of course, that he is not gun shy. Well it is now time to
nsider entering him for a trial. It must however be realised
at a dog may not run for a qualifying certificate more than
ree times in all and not more than twice in any one Field
rial Season.

When entered in a stake, if he obtains a Certificate of
erit, a setter or pointer will automatically be awarded his
ualifying certificate. If previously to the trial your dog has
en running with another dog and you know that he will not
terfere with the work of his working companion who has
en drawn to run with him, and if you think that he will
ck and not try to steal a point to put in jeopardy the
ances of the other dog to run in the second round, fair
ough, enter him in the novice stake, otherwise it would be
ir and reasonable to enter him for the qualifying certificate
ly.

Before you decide to send off the entry form, different
ctors should be considered. If the English Setter is not
ite up to the standard required yet and needs polishing,
en postpone entering him until the next season. If he is
ther too keen and not very easy to control, perhaps it
ould be wiser to enter him for the grouse trial where the
ather would certainly slow him down? but on the other
nd if your setter is not too flamboyant as one should hope,
thout any doubt he should have less difficulty in running
the Spring Trial usually held on the short vegetation of the
uth of England. Different clubs and Field Trial societies,
n various setter and pointer trials up and down the
untry. On most occasions the spring trials are held in the
uth of England, as for the Grouse Trials, the circuit which
mmences towards the beginning of the last week of July on

the English Moorlands, and in Scotland around the 12th of August when the Grouse shooting season opens. The fixtures of the trials are advertised in the Kennel Gazette from which you can obtain the addresses of the different club and society secretaries.

This chapter is not a training handbook, but I hope it might well be a guidance to any would-be handler who enjoys as I do the working side of our most attractive breed and perhaps did not possess enough information for taking the initial steps to prepare himself and his dog the the Qualifying Certificate.

8

TRIMMING, GROOMING AND SHOW PREPARATION

No book on English Setters would be complete without a chapter on trimming, for the art of the trimmer accentuates all the good points of your Setter and can, in many cases, improve points that are not the animal's best features. The most important thing to remember is that trimming is only the tip of the iceberg, the work that has gone into the dog re breeding, exercising and conditioning is of the utmost importance. The trimming of your English Setter will then add the finishing touches and your dog will look as if it has not been trimmed which is the whole secret of the art. Just, as in the chapter on showing it says that watching is worth four pages of instructions, the same can apply with trimming — go to a few shows and look how the top dogs are trimmed, and remember every skill takes a time to learn so you will not become a 'super trimmer' overnight.

First, some DO NOTS — do not leave the trimming to the night before the show, especially a 6 month old puppy who has never been touched by the scissors before. Do not use electric clippers and if you take no heed of that warning and use them, do not run the clippers down the neck, then stop at the withers, making your dog look as if he is wearing a fur poncho. Do not use blunt scissors or dirty brushes and combs, remember the truth in the saying 'a good workman looks after his tools'. This way they last longer and keep their efficiency.

From when you first bring your puppy home at 8-9 weeks, daily brushing with a soft brush is essential, for not only is it good for the coat texture and skin itself, it is invaluable in getting the puppy used to a grooming session, to standing on a table, and standing and lying quietly whilst it is done. This

is also the time for gently checking ears, teeth, paws and th
skin itself to see that nothing is amiss.

What equipment is needed? Never the electric clippers o
an English Setter you wish to show, aside from the fact tha
in the hand of the inexperienced they can become a letha
weapon. The trimmer is not barbering the Setter, jus
thinning out the hair on certain areas of the body. Brushe
the type with a strap across the back or those that look like
horse dandy brush; very useful for that brushing through a
the show the type known as a Universal brush with a handle
as long as you are not too heavy handed, is excellent. Comb
needed — a No.6, that is, about 6" in length with teeth abou
½" long, the teeth very close together. A second comb, wit
wider teeth, for combing through the feathering. Scissors –
the best you can afford to buy — one pair of sharp scissor
with fine points, one pair of thinning (serrated edge) scissors
Stripping knives that can also be used Magnet and Duplex
nail trimmers and, if you are working on your own mayb
the most important of all, a mirror large enough for you t
see the whole outline of the dog when set up. A table larg
enough for the dog to stand or lie down comfortably, with
mat to give the dog a grip. Check the table legs do no
wobble!

An English Setter for show purposes cannot be trimme
properly in a day. He must be roughed out, that is, outlin
worked out about a fortnight before the show and the
worked over a small amount at a time every day, whic
means neither you nor the dog becomes bored and th
trimmer does not become scissor happy! Remember, onc
hair is cut off it cannot be glued back on again for the nex
day. Your dog is used to the table, if you have to do the jo
on your own the dog stands quietly, easier if you have
helper, but if not a controllable dog is essential. See you hav
a good light for the operation. If artificial light, shinin
where you want it. First, brush the dog then comb through s
that there are not tags in the feathering then, using the No.
comb working from head to tail, run the comb through th
coat, paying special attention to the silky feathering on th

ears, under the ears, the feathering on the chest and the breech feathering. Be very careful not the pull any knots or tags, work them out carefully so that you do not hurt the dog. The English Setter has quite a large area of dog to be tidied so, unlike the smaller Spaniels where the finger and thumb method can be used, scissors are necessary. With the thinning (serrated) scissors remove the excess hair on the throat holding the head upwards with the left hand so that sudden movements can be anticipated, take off the rough hair from under the throat and round the neck under the ears. Remove fur just down to the breastbone — not so short that the dog's neck has a plucked appearance. When using thinning scissors always cut into the coat, never across it. Now trim the superfluous hair from the sides of the neck, holding the ear gently up so that the hair is trimmed right up to the base of the ear. The beauty of the Setter head is accentuated by the close lying ear. When trimming the underside of the ear watch carefully for the small split part of the ear, also remember how sensitive the ears are so handle gently.

Take the 'feathery' hair off the top of the ear, this helps to give the required low set ear carriage. First with the thinning scissors then, either the Magnet trimmer or Duplex, taking off the abundance of silky hair. Carefully take that line of trim up the side of the skull. I like to leave a small amount of hair on the front edge of the ear, it keeps the English Setter expression, the soft gentle one the standard requires. Where the neck merges with the shoulders see that the line does indeed merge, otherwise that lovely clean shoulder line will be lost. The rear end also needs defining, the tail can be bushy, especially where it joins the rump. The rump and rear legs can be covered with curls. The curls and extra coat from the base of the tail, comb well then, using the thinning scissors, thin cut the hair on the rump and the base of the tail, also the curls on the upper thigh. Trim extra hair away under the root of the tail so that there is a slight break between the start of the tail fringe and the rump. The finished tail should roughly be in the shape of a triangle, the tip of the tail cut with thinning scissors, cutting the end on a slant leaving about ½″ to ¾″ remaining to protect the end of the tail. The fringe trimmed to the already mentioned triangular shape. Now, from the point of hock to the foot, trim away the hair that grows outwards in a flag shape. Now to the feet which, by skillful trimming, can be given almost a new shape. Train the dog to lie down whilst foot trimming. With the straight sharp scissors cut away the tufty hair between the pads, then pull the surplus hair that grows between the toes upwards and trim with the thinning scissors. The nails ideally kept short with hard road exercise, but some nails do not wear down well even 'trot, trot, trotting on the hard, hard roads' so these must be cut, using nail cutters, as short as possible without cutting into the quick or sensitive part of the nail. It is easy to see the quick on a light coloured nail, but go very carefully with a dark nail. If you feel nervous of cutting the quick use a file to shape the nail, but that takes much longer than cutting.

The roughing out process done 2/3 weeks before the show gives the coat time to grow back into one 'piece'. In the time between the show and the roughing out, finger and thumbing is enough to keep the coat correct. Use rubber counting tips on thumb and first finger. To get a grip on the coat rub over first with chalk, the area you are going to pull. Using the fine comb and your fingers, work with little snatches, moving gradually backwards. Do this all over a few times, always keeping the hair chalked. The old dead hair comes out, leaving the new flat hair. This method does not break the hair, only thins it out. Once a dog has been trimmed, if you are showing for a consistent period, 5/10 minutes a day will keep him in show trim.

GROOMING AND SHOW PREPARATION

Trimming is dealt with in the chapter on trimming; this deals with the everyday grooming of the dog. Brush the dog once a day with a good stiff bristle brush and gently comb the feathering on legs, tail and underneath the body. This is essential so that the feathering does not tag. With regular grooming, an English Setter that is not shown does not need bathing very often, but if you show your English Setter a bath before each show will be necessary — like the television advertisements you want him 'whiter than white'. Buy a good dog shampoo, or good quality human shampoo. In the summer you can wash your dog outside, but in the winter it will be necessary to do so inside. If you have a shower on a flexible tube this is ideal, otherwise the rubber sprays are excellent. See that the floor of the bath is well covered with a rubber mat so that the dog cannot slip. Wet the dog all over except for the head. Wash with the shampoo, rinse really well, then do the head last with a flannel — remember no water down the dog's ears. You can use a conditioner if you wish; the one for humans, Clynol, is very good. Follow their instructions. Lift the dog out of the bath. Now he will shake water all over! Dry briskly with a rough towel. You want the dry dog to have a completely flat coat so either comb dry using a hair dryer rather like a hairdresser blow dries your own hair, or comb flat, then put a coat on the dog (one made of towelling is the best), leave this on till the dog is dry. If you find when you get to the show that the dog has managed to get rather dirty use Bob Martins Block Chalk or Cleansfur on the coat, but every scrape of chalk must be brushed out before the dog goes in the ring.

There are many preparations advertised for growth of hair — three that seem especially popular are Borden Mirra Coat, which is a powdered vitamin food supplement, Vita Groom a liquid coat and skin conditioner, and St. Aubrey Royal Coatalin which is applied externally to the coat.

9

MATING — BREEDING

There is a separate section on using a stud dog. The first part of this chapter deals with the bitch owner going to take his bitch to be mated. So many people join the ranks of breeders/exhibitors without ever meaning to. They buy a bitch puppy as a pet. One day, when out, somebody stops them and says "That's a lovely dog, why don't you show it?" or they see the breeder who says "She's turned out well, better than the one I've kept, show her at the local show. I will send you a schedule", and so the bug has bitten and you become part of that most absorbing of hobbies, the breeding and exhibiting of dogs. Heh! slow down, you say, we've only started showing, maybe we won't want to breed a litter. You will, there is no process as absorbing as bringing up a litter.

So you have started to show, maybe even win a little, and you decide you will breed from your bitch and keep a puppy. For the novice, selecting the sire for your proposed litter is a great problem. The aim of breeding is surely to breed an animal possessing qualities as good as the sire and dam, even superior. There are probably three main breeding systems — In-breeding of very closely related stock as sire and daughter, Mother and Son, full brother and sister. This system is best left alone by the novice; in-breeding does not cause faults, but it very quickly uncovers those lying dormant. The second system is line and family breeding. This is the mating of less closely related or family breeding. Strains and families come into being by breeders who form a pattern of carefully selected breeding, and these carry on for generations without losing any of their family characteristics. The third method could be called out-breeding, taking no notice of the characteristics of a strain, using any dog of the same breed.

In selecting the sire for your first litter, study the progeny of the dogs being shown. If you can also see the dog you fancy being shown this is excellent, but often a well known stud dog is no longer being shown, and really what the dog has sired is the most important thing, combined with the breeding of the dam of the stock you like also, at this stage, you want to use a proved sire, that is, one that has been used at stud. A line bred dog is more likely to be a dominant sire but, of course, there are exceptions and sometimes a dog who is the product of an outcross mating is a successful sire. A chance bred dog however good he is himself is unlikely to be a good sire. By chance bred, the sport of a litter, the rest very ordinary, also mediocre ancestors. All this, of course, also applies to a bitch, but more about that in the chapter on choosing your puppy.

The question of which dog to use must be well gone into before the bitch comes in season. Get it down to a short list, compare the pedigrees and then the decision. Now either speak to or write to the owner of the dog chosen. They might have a stipulation 'their dogs at stud to approved bitches only' and thus want to see your bitch. The important point is that you contact the owner of the stud dog in good time and make the arrangements, learn what the stud fee is, whether they would take a puppy in lieu of a fee, though these days the comparison between a stud fee and the price of a puppy is so much that most pay the outright fee.

MATING

Before mating the bitch must be healthy and in hard condition. The bitch comes in season at fairly regular intervals of approximately six months though often there are longer intervals in between. Often a bitch, who has always been regular, for some reason may have her heat delayed. It is often thought that the influence of light has a great effect on the mating cycle. Animals, in the wilde state, have their litters in the Spring when weather conditions are favourable and the young stock can have the advantage of the sun for growth, but man deters this way. Most bitches have two heats in the year, but this does not mean that the bitch should rear two litters a year. By doing so it is far too great a strain on her resources. Never must the bitch be regarded as a breeding machine. Remember, also, why you are mating your bitch and the fact that if things go wrong instead of making an amount of surplus money you will be spending money out on Vet's fees, etc. The first heat occurs normally between the seventh and twelfth month, though it can be a bit later in otherwise normal bitches. Most English Setters are not fully mature until they are about three years old, but they are great lasters. Though a dog matures with time, a bitch usually matures after a litter, but one should never mate a bitch too young for her to develop. The best age is about two years old. She will probably have her first heat or season as it is called at about ten months, but it can be as early as seven months or as late as eighteen months. It can vary the length of time between seasons and those who come on heat regularly every six months are in the minority — eight/nine months is common and some bitches only come in once a year. You must keep her away from male dogs for the entire three weeks of her season. It is only during the season that the normal bitch will allow herself to be mated and only then that the normal dog shows any sexual interest in her. Moreover, only during certain days (about 4/5) does mating take place. Signs to look for prior to the bitch coming into season properly. Passing water more frequently and licking herself. The vaginal orifice starts to swell and sometimes a mucous discharge. This stage can last a few days, but remember these signs can be very slight as to be barely noticeable. The season proper starts with marked swelling and discharge of blood. This may be copious, but varies with each individual — count from when you first see the blood and notify the stud dog owner. Most bitches are ready for mating between the 12/14th day. It is often written that the proper time for mating is when the red discharge has practically ceased, but this is not a rule which can always be followed, for in many bitches the red discharge will carry on throughout the entire period of the heat. Really there is only one rule for when the bitch is ready — she will tell you by her behaviour. Probably the most useful sign is the softening of the vagina and the behaviour of dogs, but the main point is she must be kept right away from other dogs for the three weeks.

Exercise is bound to be restricted for the attraction the bitch has for dogs is caused by her scent, so you do not want a queue of suiters round your front gate. Exercise carefully away from your own home on a strong collar and lead. If it is only a short journey to the stud dog arrange to take her on the twelfth day and then if she is not ready you can take her back the following day. If it is a long way it is best to then stay overnight. One should always try to accompany one's bitch. When the time comes for mating see that you have allowed your bitch to relieve herself before arriving at the stud dog's. Keep her on the lead when introducing her to the dog. Even the quietest of bitches might try to bite and snap at the dog. The procedure of mating is dealt with in the section 'The Stud Dog'. After a little time to allow the two animals to get to know each other, the stud dog owner will ask you to hold the bitch's head — both hands either side of the collar. The owner of the stud dog will probably support her under the loin in case she sits down or twists away from the dog. During the actual mating, the time of which can vary, just hold your bitch quietly. If your bitch is very difficult, snapping and refusing to stand still, the stud dog owner might ask for her to be muzzled, that is, with a nylon stocking or a leather muzzle. This is only to save the dog from being bitten and does not harm the bitch at all. Some people do not believe in forced matings and much can be said for this point of view, but some bitches would never be mated and have puppies, and some stud dogs would be bitten if a certain amount of restraint wasn't used. After the mating return the dog to the car or kennel and let her rest quietly. One mating, if the tie of normal length, should be enough. If any doubt exists about the bitch's readiness or should the tie have failed or been unduly short, a second mating can be performed. The interval between services should never be a long one — 24 hours ideal, 48 hours the limit. Conception may result from both matings, and should the interval between them be long the puppies from the second mating, born as they will be with those from the first mating, may die through their prematurity.

Stud fees should be paid at the time of mating. The stud fee is paid for the service of the dog, whether there is a litter or not. Usually the owner of the stud dog allows a second service without further fee, if no puppies result from the first mating. Stud fees vary — obviously, when the first made enquiries about using the dog you noted the fee. The stud fee is such a small item in costing a litter that one should never practise economy in this direction. The best way is, obviously, to pay the fee and that's that. Sometimes though other arrangements are made, if so, state them in writing. Especially, if one or more puppies are to be taken in lieu of the fee, it should be definitely stated which choice, if any, the owner of the sire is to have. Cover also the contingency of only one puppy! The owner of the stud dog has certain responsibilities — it is a moral obligation that the dog shall be fertile and a proved sire, unless it is clearly understood that the mating is an experimental one. If the bitch is left in his charge he assumes responsibility for her.

THE STUD DOG

Many people think what they can save in stud fees if they have their own stud dog, also what he will make in stud fees, but basically it often does not work out like this. You can choose any dog in the country, any blood lines, any famous champion you wish to use. Probably, unless your dog wins very well, very few bitches will come to him, but here are a few hints if you do want to use your own dog. Fo his first mating try to get an experienced bitch who knows what it is all about and is easily mated. It is not advisable to try a maiden bitch. Do not use a young dog too much at stud. His first bitch when he is between 12/15 months. Do not feed your dog just before he mates a bitch and see that both animals have relieved themselves. Introduce both animals on collars and leads. A reasonable amount of space to be used with non-slip floor. An experienced bitch will encourage the dog by moving her tail and generally flirting. Encourage the dog to mount the bitch and from the beginning get your dog used to your helping him by supporting the bitch under the loin in case she suddenly sits down. Do not rush things, the early flirting is important to relax the bitch. The supporting of the bitch is important, just as it is important that the owner of the bitch holds her head firmly so she cannot turn and snap at the dog. When the dog first penetrates the bitch it may be painful and the bitch attempt to move away. Hold them firmly. The dog will clasp her round the abdomen with his forelegs — keep them like this for about 10 seconds so the tie has chance to start. The dog will then be ready to turn — he can be helped to do so by lifting one foreleg over the bitch's back so that both are on the same side, then the corresponding hindleg lifted gently over the bitch's hindquarters — the two are then standing back to back. They must be kept steady for the length of the tie which can be from 10 minutes to 1 hour. A small stool is a good idea for the stud dog's owner who can clasp the dog and bitch together by sitting on the stool in the middle. When the dog withdraws, the bitch should be taken away to rest, the dog washed underneath with weak disinfectant and put back in the kennel. Do not let a dog spend too long trying unsuccessfully to mate a bitch. Give him a rest for half-an-hour and then let him try again.

10

CARE OF THE IN-WHELP BITCH AND WHELPING

After your bitch has been mated and finished her season she can return to her normal and regular exercise, but I would recommend that you do not go travelling her miles to shows. In whelp and nursing bitches should have plenty of meat and milk, plus additional vitamins. It is not necessary to increase the amount of food for the first four weeks, so the ideal is a plentiful supply of meat, a good wholemeal cereal, and such additions as eggs, Cod Liver or Halibut Liver Oil, and extra bone forming material. I use Calcidee tablets for extra calcium, for in whelp bitches there are many excellent preparations for extra calcium which you can buy. Remember, it is quality not quantity, plenty of protein foods, cut down on the carbohydrate foods. Sometimes bitches become fussy about their food when in whelp. If so, try to tempt her with something different. She must have extra protein — if all else fails Casilan mixed with something she will eat. As pregnancy goes forward the unborn puppies grow very quickly; from five weeks onward your bitch's appetite will increase — give 1½/2 lbs. meat a day plus additives. As the bitch gets heavier, it is often wiser to divide the food into three meals daily which is much more comfortable for the bitch. You should not allow the bitch to become too fat, fatness can lead to difficult whelpings. Old stockmen used to say that a bitch who puts all her food 'on her own back' does not nurture her puppies as well as one who remains rounded, but not over-fat. Keep up regular exercise until the bitch gets heavy and will not want to walk herself for any distance — see she takes a little exercise every day — do not take her car rides after five weeks. This is no hard and fast rule, but usually it is possible to say that a bitch is definitely in whelp between five and six weeks after mating. Early signs in a maiden bitch — her teats often enlarge and go rather pink by about three weeks. Sometimes they start to take great care of themselves and stop playing with other dogs.

WHELPING

The period of gestation is nine weeks and enclosed in this book is a table showing when a bitch is due to whelp. Maiden bitches or those carrying a large litter can whelp quite safely as much as six days early. Older bitches who have had previous litters and those with small litters frequently whelp late. I should advise that if your bitch shows no sign of having her puppies by the 65th day consult your veterinary surgeon. If, at any time during the 63 days she has been restless or ill, or has a blackish discharge, or if she starts whelping more than five days early, then call your vet.

You have obviously decided well before the great day where your bitch will have her puppies. Somewhere where she will be happy and at ease, for tranquility is part of an easy whelping. If it is in the house it must be somewhere quiet and let her spend some time there each day for about a fortnight before she is due. If she lives in a kennel with other dogs a separate compartment away from the other dogs. The whelping box which, when made, can be used time and time again is so important. In any whelping box there must be room for the bitch to lie comfortably with plenty of space for the litter, for the box is used for both as long as the puppies are in the nest. The box should be about 4½ feet square. During whelping and, for about a week afterwards, a moveable rail similar to the pig rail of a farmer, can be fitted 5½" high and about the same distance from the sides of the box. Brush handles, if you make the box yourself, are ideal. These rails stop puppies, if the crawl behind the dam, being squashed when she lies down. Make the sides about 18" high, the front should be three separate boards that can be taken out one at a time — just one board in when the bitch first uses it so she does not have to jump; the other boards can be put in as the puppies get older. Temperature during the time of birth and for the first few weeks is most important. Puppies born inside during the summer will need no artificial heat, but even in the summer the nights can be cold for kennel puppies. In the winter even inside the temperature can be lower than one thinks. Puppies thrive and are contented with an infra-red lamp hung over the box, the dull emitter type or those that give a red glow, but not the bright ones. Have the chain with plenty of slack because after a couple of days you might want to take it higher; 75° for the first 24 hours then 65°. Have the lamp hanging about 3′ above the box. If there is no electricity, oil heaters can be used, but be careful that it cannot be knocked over and that it is kept clean and will not smoke. Collect plenty of newspaper for the whelping and afterwards when you are really using it — newspaper disappears like snow in summer. Newspaper is an ideal medium on the floor of the box when whelping, when dirty it can be burnt and puppies cannot crawl underneath. The amount of supervision one gives a whelping bitch depends very much on her temperament and yours. Fussiness is not needed, but quiet supervision there must be or the bitch may endure unnecessary suffering and puppies die. A maiden bitch must be watched well, especially when she has started to strain because it is only by being there at the beginning that one knows in time if all is not going well. The best is to stay with the bitch from when she starts to strain until the last puppy is born, but this can be for a long spell for the last puppy can be born some time after the others.

Preparations for Whelping done well in advance; your Vet knowing what day the bitch is due; rough towels, cotton wool, Dettol and sterilized scissors all ready. Signs that whelping is imminent — no desire to take food, the puppies seem to be carried lower down, the Vulva will be softer and swollen and a thick whitish sticky discharge. If you take her temperature it will be below normal from 101.4° to 99°. If the bitch's temperature is normal she is not likely to whelp for 24 hours. The fall is probably a natural method of preparing the puppies for the change in temperature which

Sh. Ch. Elswood White
Heatherette

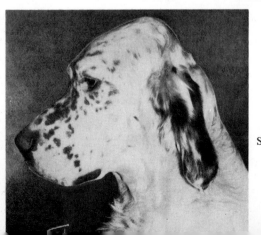

Sh. Ch. Fencefoot Freckler

Sh. Ch. Silbury Soames of Madavale

Ch. Upperwood Zoe

Sh. Ch. Jewel of Thrumall

Sh. Ch. Clariho W. of V.R.

happens at birth. The bitch will become restless and start scratching about in her box. If loose in the garden she might start to dig a hole. We had one bitch who decided a cucumber frame was the ideal maternity unit! Stage I, when whelping begins in earnest, the bitch will pant and turning round look at her tail and lick herself, and start the irregular and spasmodic contraction of the uterine muscle. As soon as the genital passages are dilated the main stage of labour Stage II starts. It is a good idea to have a warm hot water bottle ready in a cardboard box with a towel over it; the size of the box you get your groceries in will do. Contractions, like ripples, pass down the bitch's sides. Make a note of the time these contractions first start — if no puppy within two hours call your Veterinary Surgeon. Usually the first puppy will be born about half-an-hour after the contractions start. The lowest lying puppy is gradually forced through the passage. The first thing you notice is the bag of membranes or water bag protruding from the Vulva. This contains fluid to aid the birth of the puppy — it finally bursts, releasing the fluid it contains — membranes may not break until after the head is born, if so, they must be broken in order that the puppy may breathe. The puppies are encased in a membrane which the bitch will tear, she will then lick the puppy all over and get him breathing. She will bite the umbilical cord which attaches the puppy to the after-birth and then probably eat the after-birth. This is quite natural and contains what is of use to the bitch. If the bitch is a maiden and just does not seem to know what to do push the puppy towards her head and try to get her to lick it. No time must be wasted if the bitch still does nothing; break the film at the pup's mouth, removing the mucous, which will enable it to breathe and expand the lungs for the first time. Once the placenta has separated the puppy must breathe or die. A maiden bitch may not attempt to bite through the cord of the first puppy, if so, wait half-a-minute to enable as much blood as possible to enter the puppy's circulation from the cord, gently squeeze the cord flat, pressing blood towards the puppy, and then cut with sterilized scissors about 2″ from the puppy. Never pull the cord away from the stomach as you will cause a hernia. Then, place the puppy back between the dam's front paws and she will lick the puppy dry — the action of the tongue serves to stimulate the puppy. The length of time a bitch takes to have a litter varies. They may have them very quickly, in many cases fifteen to thirty minutes elapse between the births. Sometimes several are born on each others heels and then a gap occurs. There is no need to worry unless she continues to strain without any result. Remember always call the Vet if she has strained for two hours without a puppy being born. During whelping give liquid little and often, a drink of warm milk and Glucodin or Honey, and if she is getting tired add a teaspoonful of Brandy. Should the puppies be left with the bitch while the rest of the litter is being born? Everybody seems to have different ideas on this — it really depends on the bitch. Let the puppies find a nipple and start suckling the bitch will lick them which is all to the good, but when she is actually have another puppy, place them in the box on the warm hot water bottle. If she frets whilst they are away leave her with them. It is never easy to be sure when the bitch has finished, English Setters have reasonably large litters, but twelve is a very large litter so, if after a few slight strains to clear herself, she starts to clean herself up and then settle down to a sleep. If, after an hour she seems quite peaceful, put the puppies into the hot water box, take the bitch out to relieve herself (ideal if somebody else can do this), change the papers in the box, when the bitch returns settle her in the clean box with puppies. Give her a drink, dry her feathering a little, but do not wash it. Leave her to rest for 2/3 hours, take her temperature when you come back, and if it is over 103° the day after whelping, consult your Vet in case it means a retained after-birth or a dead puppy. Other signs of this are restlessness, straining and not bothering with the puppies. Most bitches do not want to leave their puppies at first when they need to relieve themselves, but they must do so, if necessary, put a lead on to take them into the garden. During the first week/ten days there will be a good deal of blood-stained discharge, this blood and mucous should stop; if it starts to show traces of pus it is a sign the Vet's help is needed — modern antibiotics have an amazing effect in no time at all. The bitch will probably have Diarrhoea for the first day or two, her motions will be copious and black, which is usually caused by the placentas eaten. Keep her on milk foods for the first forty-eight hours. If needed your Vet will give you something to control the Diarrhoea. After forty-eight hours you can gently wash the stained feathering, but towel it dry.

Feeding of the nursing bitch is mentioned in the chapter on feeding.

I have, in a footnote to this chapter, mentioned a few things which can go wrong, but on the whole English Setters are good whelpers.

UTERINE INERTIA

The name given to a condition in which the normal powerful uterine contractions, which push out the puppy, are either very weak or none at all. The uterine activity which precedes birth is largely dependent on the stimuli induced by the alteration in the hormone balance of the bitch's blood stream. Usually injection of uterine stimulant like Pituitrin, is effective. If a bitch, which appears to be suffering from uterine inertia does not respond reasonably quickly to Pituitrin a Caesarian operation should not be delayed. Another form of inertia can be caused by exhaustion of the uterine muscle, following excessive activity; this can be caused by an obstructed labour, that is, abnormally large puppy, faulty position of a puppy, in which case Pituitrin would be useless. No stimulus to contraction can help if the delay is an insuperable obstacle. Again Caesarian section. A Caesarian operation will save your puppies and bitch when undertaken at an early stage, when the bitch is in good condition. Uterine inertia, it is thought, could be of genetic origin.

ECLAMPSIA

Due to lack of Calcium in the blood, can occur after

whelping when the puppies are suckling and large amounts of Calcium have been given in the milk. Signs to be noticed — stiffness in the hind legs, followed by convulsions. Call the Vet immediately who will inject Calcium Salts whereupon the recovery is like a miracle.

HAEMORRHAGE

Can occur after the puppies have been born safely. If blood is coming away from the bitch, fresh red blood, again call the Vet. It may be caused because the uterus has lost the power to contract and the uterus then fills with blood from the placental sites. It may be caused by coagulation defect, that is, a failure for one reason or another in the blood clotting mechanism.

11

CARE OF A NURSING BITCH AND HER PUPPIES

The bitch, with her puppies, needs privacy. After 48 hours on milk foods only, give fish or mince for one meal; add porridge oats or brown bread to one milk meal. Eggs are excellent protein value and tripe can be used too. Meat can be given after three days. By the end of the week she can have really as much as she wants — 2 lbs. of meat (given in two meals) — four meals altogether. Milk and Honey + Farex — a cereal in the morning — the meat at mid-day — meat and meal at 4.00 p.m. — milk at night plus the extra additives, which must be given until the puppies are completely weaned. The bitch needs, at this time, a high protein diet — she will then feed her puppies without depleting her own resources. Remember, the well being and development of the litter depends on the amount and quality of the dam's milk. Clean drinking water must be available at all times. Ample feeding should continue for the first four to five weeks, after which the amounts can be gradually reduced as the puppies begin to feed themselves. By the time they are weaned the dam's diet should be back to normal. Examine the milk glands every day — the teats not used will become congested. (This often happens with a small litter). If the gland feels hard and lumpy gently massage it. Milk the teat then put a puppy on to feed from it.

If the puppies are under an infra-red lamp raise it slightly during the day so as to keep the temperature as even as possible, also to harden the puppies, at first raise the lamp, then turn it off during the hottest part of the day and off altogether by the time they are ready to go to their new homes. Puppies start to open their eyes at about nine days old, but they are not opened properly until they are about a

fortnight old. Until then keep them in a dim light. At a
fortnight old cut their sharp little nails — the tip with very
sharp scissors. If you do not do this they will scratch the bitch
and make her disinclined to let them feed.

WEANING

It has been said that what a puppy eventually becomes as
an adult depends almost as much on its feeding and rearing
as on its breeding. One example is the ability to grow bone of
a certain substance and quality. This is, of course, a
hereditary characteristic due to the fact that if the genetic
factors for good bone formation are not there no amount of
extra feeding with minerals and vitamins will produce it.
Correct feeding and rearing from weaning time to maturity
are essential if maximum potential bone, size and strength is
to be developed. If a bitch has sufficient milk the puppies will
obtain all their nourishment from their dam for the first
three weeks of their lives. At the end of that time the first
teeth will be piercing the gums and supplementary feeding
may start. As a beginning puppies must be taught to lap.
Heat some milk to blood heat. Place some in a saucer or on
to a tablespoon, take each puppy one at a time, hold the
saucer or the spoon up to the puppy, and put it towards the
puppy. Many lap at once, others blow and suck before they
get the knack, but they all learn to lap in a very short time.
Use one of the preparatory brands of milk food –
unmodified cows milk has only one third of the nutritive
value of bitches' milk and the puppy would be dangerously
distended on cows milk obtaining the actual amount of
nourishment needed. Goats milk is good and, if you can
enrich cows milk to the required strength, but it is just as
good to use the right powdered milk — Lactol is excellent. If
for some reason, the puppies do not seem to thrive and do
not gain weight as you weigh them each day, because the
dam's milk seems inadequate, buy a premature baby's
feeding bottle and give them supplementary feeds. If, for
some reason, they cannot feed off the bitch you must hand
rear them. It can be done — we did it once with a litter of nine

whose dam died when the puppies were 10 days old. Warmth is the first essential — feeds should be two-hourly, night and day, for the first week, then gradually reduce to longer intervals. The most important thing in hand rearing is keeping the puppies' bowels working. For the first few days of life puppies pass water only when stimulated by the bitch's licking, so if there is no bitch it is essential after every feed that the puppy's tummy is massaged with cotton wool soaked in Olive Oil, then cleaned up gently. With a normal litter, start to give at three weeks one milk meal so that they are lapping really well by the time they are four weeks old. At four weeks give them each a teaspoonful of raw scraped meat. Put a little bit in the puppy's mouth and he will probably eat it straight away. After a week minced meat can be used. Also at four weeks one milk meal and one milk and Farex, and about 1½ oz. meat per puppy. At five weeks two milk, one plus Farex, one of meat or fish — fish must always be cooked. The bitch is now away from her pups for quite long sessions and will feed them morning, mid-day and evening. She might also try to vomit her food back for the puppies. No real starchy foods added until the puppies are about six weeks old. By six weeks the puppies can be independent of the bitch altogether.

Try to feed the puppies individually or in two's, so that the greediest do not get more than their share. The following is a suitable guide for feeding six week old puppies:

7.30 a.m./ 8.30 a.m.:	Prepared Milk and Farex or Farlene. Honey is exellent also in this feed.
Noon:	Minced meat (cooked, if necessary). A broken up fish mixed with a little fine puppy meal which has been well soaked in gravy, Oxo, Marmite, Kenedex.
2.00 p.m.:	Bitch to visit her puppies.
5.00 p.m.:	Milk Feed.
8.00 p.m.:	Meat.
10.00 p.m./ 11.00 p.m.	Bitch to be returned for the night.

The bitch should now have a bed which the puppies cannot reach. When the puppies are 7 weeks old the bitch will have very little milk left. In any case, as the puppies can go to their new homes when eight weeks old they should then be completely weaned. Amounts of food should be steadily increased — a growing puppy needs more food for its weight than an adult — bones are hardening and muscles developing. By eight weeks each puppy is having four ounces of meat, (twice a day), one pint of reconstituted milk plus additives, 4 ozs. meal, etc. These are average amounts and can be increased if puppies look thin, or decreased if their stomachs bulge too much. Offer the puppies fresh water every day. At six weeks onward place feeding bowls on bricks so that the dogs' front is helped by standing up to their food.

Puppies can be wormed for the first time at four weeks, second time at seven weeks. Get the worming preparation from your Vet and follow the directions completely.

For the first few days after the puppies are born the bitch stays in the box with them, even her food can be held there for her to eat. Later, after she has fed the puppies, she will spend short periods outside the box. Up to when the puppies are three weeks old keep the moveable boards up on the front of the box, then when you want the puppies out of the box and moving round, remove the front boards so that the puppies can just walk out. Sawdust on the floor. The bitch should have a bed where she can go if she wants to get away from the puppies. When you start feeding the puppies always feed them before the bitch goes back. From the end of the fifth week start to decrease the bitch's food, so that her milk dries up gradually and she keeps in good condition.

A puppy can be sent on a train at eight weeks and can do without food for twelve hours, but I am afraid that unless it is a direct train I view it with suspicion. For puppies going abroad, an animal freight expert will deal with all your problems — Ryslip Kennels, Binfield, Berks., are excellent in this respect. When you hand the puppy over to the new owner always give a diet sheet, pedigree form and registration certificate, together with transfer form from the

ennel Club. The Kennel Club deal with so many
gistrations, send off your form, registering the litter in
enty of time.

English Setter Puppy Diet for an eight week old puppy:

reakfast: 1/3 pint warm milk mixed with either Farex
or Farlene, Porridge — heaped tablespoon of
Honey or Glucodin.

unch: 6 oz. Minced Beef (start cutting into cubes — 7
weeks) mixed with 1 large breakfast cup of
Wholemeal Puppy Meal soaked in Oxo,
Marmite, Bovril, Kenedex Stock, either 1 tsp.
Stress or 1 Calcidee Tablet.

ea: 1/3 pint warm milk.
Bonio Rusks to gnaw.

upper: Repeat of lunch — instead of meat give fish —
if bones, cooked and mashed. Pilchards in
Tomato Sauce seem to be a special favourite.

Drink of milk can be given before bed.
Vetzyme Tablets — two a day.
Give powdered milk up to puppy being ten weeks old, then
cows milk. Egg yolk is also good.
Increase meat and meal as puppy grows.
Adult English Setter should have 1½ lbs. of meat per day;
¾/1 lb. meal; 1 pint milk. Four meals a day until three
months, increasing meat, etc., each week by ½ oz. per day
until 1½ lbs. is reached.
Decrease to three meals a day at three months.
Decrease to two meals a day at six months.
Decrease to one meal a day at nine months.
At three months — 2 Calcidee Tablets.
Change to wholemeal terrier meal.
Vegetables can be put into the stock pot at 3½/4½
months.

When teething the puppy can go off his food. Bonios Marrow Bones with no splinters (sawn not chopped) seem help.

If puppies get Diarrhoea, there used to be a wonder paste called Vansup which was obtainable from G.P. Male Partners, Westcroft, Earley, Reading, Berks.

The value of a change in diet should never be overlooke Dogs can become bored with the same food all the time

AN ALPHABET OF AILMENTS

Anal Glands

If you see your dog dragging himself along on the grou on his hindquarters, his anal glands probably need attentic These glands are either side of the rectum and occasiona need squeezing out. At first take him to the Veterina Surgeon to have it done until you have learned the corre way to do it.

Canker

A term often used to cover various affections of the e Veterinary attention with anything wrong with the e Panalog made by E.R. Squibb & Sons Ltd., has cured ma Setters of ear complaints.

Cough

A virus infection. The cough, which lasts for 6/8 weeks very catching to other animals so no shows. Old fashion linctus or sugar and Friars Balsam which gives a relievi vapour at the back of the dog's throat.

Diabetes

Two types — general symptoms, great thirst/drin excessively, loses weight, passes a great amount of urir Often accompaniment of a disease of the Kidneys. Must treated by a Veterinary Surgeon.

Distemper (Infectious Hepatitis and Leptospiroses)

Nowadays, dogs are protected by inoculation from

weeks against these infectious diseases, which are highly infectious. The first symptoms are dullness, loss of appetite, vomiting and diarrhoea, weepy eyes, discharge from the nose, and a rise in temperature.

Haemorrhage

Can occur after whelping. English Setters may suffer from a form of Haemophilia, the disease that Queen Victoria passed through her daughters to most of the Royal Houses of Europe. Research has shown that in pregnancy and immediately after delivery a specific type of coagulation defect may occur in the female's blood. Haemorrhagic blood is bright red, and if the bitch continues to lose blood in a heavy flow call your Veterinary Surgeon who will give her an injection to cause the blood to clot.

Hip-Dysplasia

A congenital abnormality of the hip joint. Found in English Setters. First recognised in dogs in the 1930's, it is a hereditary defect. Can only be diagnosed by competent X-raying. In some cases Hip-Dysplasia may not cause problems until old age when osteoarthritic changes occur. If systems are so severe even as a puppy, that is, poor gait in the hind legs, weakness in back legs, excessive sideways movement of the hips. Reluctance to jump even small obstacles,the dog tires easily and sits rather than stands, shows discomfort when rising, and can cry out in pain if it lies in an uncomfortable position. If the animal is in pain because of this defect there is really only one solution, it should be put to sleep. However, if the animal is not in pain it can lead an active life and adjust itself to the defect. Animals, which have been X-rayed and found to be badly malformed, should not be used for breeding purposes.

Pancreatic Deficiency

Symptoms similar to diabetes, classic symptom, passing large quantities of faecal material. Simply, the pancreas is not doing its work in helping with its enzymes to digest the food. Tablets, like Panteric, prescribed by your Veterinary

Surgeon, will put the matter right and, in some cases, seem t
effect a cure.

Parasites
1. Fleas, bugs and mites. Can be caught by the best looke
   after animals. Alugan made by Hoechst Pharmaceuticals
   in spray or powder form, for bathing, is excellent.

2. Mange. Two types, common or sarcoptic, on which yo
   can use Alugan, and follicular in which the mites live o
   and in the skin. It is very difficult to cure and veterinar
   treatment is needed.

Worms
   Roundworms — found in puppies, and if puppies are no
wormed they will retard puppies' progress, thus they must b
wormed whether worms are apparent or not at 4/5 weeks
Your Veterinary Surgeon will supply the tablets.
   Tapeworms — usually affect adult dogs. Segments can b
seen in the motions/small, grey-white, seed-like objects
Dogs with tapeworms tend to have a big appetite, but do no
put on weight, and have dull coats. Obtain Tapeworm
tablets, dose accordingly. Burn the resulting excreta.

12

SHOWS

There are five types of shows held under Kennel Club Rules. Your dog must be registered at the Kennel Club to be shown at all, except Exemption Shows.

1. *Exemption Shows*
Usually run in conjunction with another event. Have about four classes for pedigree dogs only and several novelty classes. Entries taken at the show.

2. *Sanction Shows*
Small shows of twenty classes. Confined to members. Not many breed classes. Probably have to enter Any Variety Setter or Any Variety Gundog. No dogs which have won a Challenge Certificate are eligible and the highest class is Post-Graduate i.e. for dogs which have not won more than five first prizes at Championship Shows and Open Shows in Post-Graduate, Minor-Limit, Mid-Limit and Open Classes. Entries usually close a fortnight before the show. The dogs are not benched and stay with their owners.

3. *Limited Shows*
Confined also to members and limited to dogs who have not won a Challenge Certificate. Usually have more than twenty classes and might have some breed classes.

4. *Open Shows*
Open to all dogs and all exhibitors. Can be benched. Usually, nowadays some English Setter Classes. Excellent training ground for novice dog and novice exhibitor.

5. *Championship Shows*

The peak of the dog showing tree. Held all over the Country divided into General Championship Shows. Breed Clubs also hold Championship Shows and so do Group Breed Shows. Always benched. It is at these shows that the Kennel Club Challenge Certificates are awarded, one for each sex, and to become a Champion a dog must win three Challenge Certificates under three different judges, provided that at least one of the Challenge Certificates was awarded when the dog was more than 12 months old. In English Setters and all Gundog breeds it is necessary to obtain a qualifying certificate at a field trial to become a full Champion. Without a qualifying certificate a gundog takes the title of Show Champion (abbreviated to Sh. Ch.) English Setters have certificates at every general championship show, except Belfast and, in addition, have two Breed Club Ch. Shows, and two group shows give us C C's. Breed Shows are the best place to bring out puppies otherwise quiet Open Shows are good. To find out where the shows are being held and who to write to for a schedule obtain one or both of the weekly dog papers — "Our Dogs"/"Dog World", full also of interesting information plus notes about your breed. The larger shows have many classes restricted by age or wins — read carefully, the class definitions really are self-explanatory.

Get to the show in good time. Take a show bag with grooming equipment and a bench blanket for your dog to lie on, If a benched show a bench chain to attach to his collar. A show lead to wear in the ring, at the bigger shows there are stalls selling all these things and more, brush and comb for final grooming, chalk or cleansfur in case he gets dirty on the way to the show, rubbed over then well brushed out. Water and milk in plastic bottles and a dish for him to drink out of. When you get there ask where the English Setters are benched. Then after benching your dog find where the ring is, the steward, once judging starts, at the time stated will announce the order of the classes. The Judge will tell you how he wishes you to move your dog, remember a steady trot when moving your dog (it's not a race). Oh don't forget to take a pin to put your exhibitors number on with. Competition is very keen in English Setters so don't be disappointed if you don't get into the cards at your first show. As well as beauty classes some shows have obedience classes and certain clubs are for obedience work only. Up to now English Setters have never produced an Obedience Champion. There are special Field Trials run for Setters and Pointers, see chapter Field — Training.

13

'potted' BIOGRAPHIES OF SOME WELL KNOWN KENNELS

Some biographical details of the Kennels whose prefixes and affixes you might find in your puppy's pedigree. This is not a comprehensive list; I have written about those who have been and are still involved over the last ten years. This is a handbook so is, of necessity, curtailed in size so I apologise, but make no mention of the Rombalds of the Crowthers, Miss M. Jarry's Ripleygaes, Mrs. Jocelyn English's great Shiplakes (she bred or owned 18 Ch's. or Sh. Ch's.), and Mrs. A. Broadhead's famous Ernfords. These prefixes are still found in your pedigrees, alas Mr. & Mrs. Crowther are dead and the three latter kennels no longer breed and show.

Suntop — Miss Margaret Barnes. The Suntop English Setters have been bred and shown since 1949. Previous to that the prefix for Cocker Spaniels was owned by Miss Barnes's Mother. The first British title holder was Ch. Suntop Suzette of Sewerby made up in 1953, but the present day Suntops are built upon Ch. Suntop Carnival Queen and her son Suntop Songbird bred by Capt. Kendall. Songbird, winner of Junior Warrant and 9 Res. C.C.'s indeed a champion manque, sired 6 Sh. Champions and has been one of the most influential sires of the post war period. Other title holders, bred or owned by this kennel, Sh.Ch. Suntop Royalbird, Sh.Ch. Suntop Royal Sunglint, Sh.Ch. Suntop Royal Sunrise, Sh.Ch. Suntop Seabird, Sh.Ch. Suntop Snowbird, Sh.Ch. Flatford Why Wonder, Sh.Ch. Suntop Bluethrush, Sh.Ch. Suntop Bluewings, Sh.Ch. Suntop Winter Breeze, another great stud force Suntop Winterbird, still in the Suntop Kennels, sire to date of 7 Sh. Champions. The Suntops have been one of the two kennels that over the last 15 years have most influenced the breed.

Iroquois — Mrs. Lesley Allan-Scott and, latterly, also her daughter, Mrs. A. Bolton. Started in 1946, first big winner Iroquois Carissima tragically killed. Great foundation bitch, Iroquois Ernford Irresistible, dam of three show champions. Show Champions owned or bred by this kennel Sh.Ch. Prince Charming of Ketree (in partnership with Mr. B. McNally), Sh.Ch. Iroquois Casanova, Sh.Ch. Iroquois Stormcloud, Sh.Ch. Iroquois Strathspey — these four dogs have been influential sires as well as winners. Sh.Ch. Iroquois Bluemoon, Sh.Ch. Iroquois Cascade, Sh.Ch. Iroquois Courtesan, Sh.Ch. Iroquois Cointreau, Sh.Ch. Iroquois Rainbow, Sh.Ch. Iroquois Solitaire, Sh.Ch. Iroquois Mooncloud and Sh.Ch. Iroquois Whiteseal Silvermorn. The second great kennel which, over the last 15 years, has influenced the progress of the breed.

Engsett — Mr. & Mrs. H. Wheeler. Breeding and showing since 1949. The foundation of the kennel the C.C. Winners Irisit Saucy Sue and Shiplake. Hemlington Spotlight 9 Res. C.C.'s. Sh.Champions, bred or owned, Sh.Ch. Engsett Exception, Sh.Ch. Engsett Elect, Sh.Ch. Engsett Electrode (a great sire and show dog), Sh.Ch. Engsett Enchantress of Fiveacres, Sh.Ch. Engsett Brilliance, Sh.Ch. Fenman Fragrance and Sh.Ch. Bournehouse Enchantress.

Elswood — The Late Mr. W. Foss and Mrs. Foss. Started in 1943 with the purchase of a bitch puppy who, when Championship Shows were resumed after the war, became Sh.Ch. Pamina of Ketree, followed by Rombalds Revel who won the first Dog Challenge Certificate after the war. Sh.Ch. Elswood Blue Lady, Sh.Ch. Elswood Dotterel, Sh.Ch. Elswood Renmark Baronet (sire of 5 Sh.Ch.'s), Sh.Ch. Elswood Ashpenda Moonquest, Sh.Ch. Elswood White Heatherette, Sh.Ch. Elswood Highlight.

Hurwyn — Mrs. S.E. Wilkinson. Started in 1949 by Mrs. Wilkinson's Mother, Mrs. C. Wilson, and owned in partnership until Mrs. Wilson's death. First big winner Hurwyn Rainbow. Two C.C.'s. Bred the influential brother and sister, Sh.Ch. Iroquois Stormcloud and Sh.Ch.

Trodgers Hurwyn Heavan. Further title holders, owned and bred, Sh.Ch. Hurwyn Morning Glory, Sh.Ch. Hurwyn All Glory, Sh.Ch. Hurwyn Wigeon, Sh.Ch. Suford Hurwyn Whinchat.

Trodgers — Mrs. A.M. Tate. Amongst so many good ones — Sh.Ch. Trodgers Meadow Fescue, one of the best bitches since the war, Sh.Ch. Trodgers Hurwyn Heavan, Trodgers Oragon — 2 C.C.'s, Kayswood Trodgers Buckwheat — 1 C.C., Sh.Ch. Trodgers Impala, Sh.Ch. Trodgers Scots Oat (Best Gundog Crufts), and Sh.Ch. Trodgers Bluebell.

Ashpenda — Mrs. C. Duffield. Foundation puppy became a famous winner and great dam, Sh.Ch. Iroquois Bluemoon. Bred Sh.Ch. Iroquois Solitaire, Sh.Ch. Elswood Ashpenda Moonquest, Sh.Ch. Ashpenda Red Robin, Sh.Ch. Ashpenda Kittiwake, the C.C. winner, Ashpenda Golden Pheasant.

Bournehouse — Mr. G.F. Williams. Started with Eveningflight of Frejendor, bred by Mrs. D.Borrowdale whose Frejendor's were well known after the war. Eveningflight won 2 C.C.'s (one at Crufts), mated to his owner's Iroquois Jasmine, produced Sh.Ch. Bournehouse Meadowfern (who was the dam of Ch.Ch. Bournehouse Enchantress), and Sh.Ch. Bournehouse Ballerina, a famous winner. Also bred by Mr. Williams — Sh.Ch. Barrenco Bournehouse Diorama, Sh.Ch. Bournehouse Figaro, and the dual C.C. Winner Bournehouse Flirting Freda.

Mawdsley — Mr. T.W. Watkinson. The fountain head of many northern kennels. Owned or bred by this kennel — Ch. Raycroft Jewel, C.C. Winner Raycroft Orange Boy, Ch. Mawdsley Lisette of Langlea, Sh.Ch. Mawdsley Ladybird of Barningham, Sh.Ch. Jewel of Thrumall, Sh.Ch. Suntop Royal Mark of Etherwood and Sh.Ch. Hepton Mawdsley Aloysius.

Silbury — Mr. & Mrs. P. Gardiner-Swann. The kennel was founded in 1949. Not only are the dogs shown, but Mr. Gardiner-Swann shoots over them. Bred the immortal Sh.Ch. Silbury Soames of Madavale winner of 24 C.C.'s and Supreme B.I.S. Crufts, and his little sister Sh.Ch. Redtops

Silbury Sonya and the C.C. winner Silbury Seeker.

Old Holbans — Mrs. A. Findlay. Has proved an influential kennel in the breed. Bred or owned — Sh.Ch. Oldholbans Pirate, Sh.Ch. Iroquois Cointreau and Sh.Ch. Oldholbans Dill.

Boisdale — Founded prior to the war. Mrs. M. Darling also trained and handled her English Setter Champions. Title holders since the war. Champion Boisdale Buttercup, Boisdale Butterfly 2 C.C.'s Qualifying Certificate, and Ch. Boisdale Puffin.

This list is, of necessity, short but Mr. & Mrs. Upton (Gorsebrook), Mrs. J. Thomas (Attleford), Miss D.E. Jones (Grelancot), Mrs. H.W. Martin (Wolvershill), Mr. & Mrs. S. Boulton (Ednasid), and Mr. & Mrs. R. Gortonbe (Upperwood), Mrs. Y. Rudin (Suford), Mrs. M. Neave (Renmark) Miss Foster-Barham (Coritan) and Mrs. N. Treharne (Redtops) are just a few more breeders who spring to mind.

TABLE SHOWING WHEN A BITCH IS DUE TO WHELP

Srvd Jan	Due to Whlp Mar	Srvd Fed	Due to Whlp Apr	Srvd Mar	Due to Whlp May	Srvd Apr	Due to Whlp Jun	Srvd May	Due to Whlp Jul	Srvd Jun	Due to Whlp Aug
1	5	1	5	1	3	1	3	1	3	1	3
2	6	2	6	2	4	2	4	2	4	2	4
3	7	3	7	3	5	3	5	3	5	3	5
4	8	4	8	4	6	4	6	4	6	4	6
5	9	5	9	5	7	5	7	5	7	5	7
6	10	6	10	6	8	6	8	6	8	6	8
7	11	7	11	7	9	7	9	7	9	7	9
8	12	8	12	8	10	8	10	8	10	8	10
9	13	9	13	9	11	9	11	9	11	9	11
10	14	10	14	10	12	10	12	10	12	10	12
11	15	11	15	11	13	11	13	11	13	11	13
12	16	12	16	12	14	12	14	12	14	12	14
13	17	13	17	13	15	13	15	13	15	13	15
14	18	14	18	14	16	14	16	14	16	14	16
15	19	15	19	15	17	15	17	15	17	15	17
16	20	16	20	16	18	16	18	16	18	16	18
17	21	17	21	17	19	17	19	17	19	17	19
18	22	18	22	18	20	18	20	18	20	18	20
19	23	19	23	19	21	19	21	19	21	19	21
20	24	20	24	20	22	20	22	20	22	20	22
21	25	21	25	21	23	21	23	21	23	21	23
22	26	22	26	22	24	22	24	22	24	22	24
23	27	23	27	23	25	23	25	23	25	23	25
24	28	24	28	24	26	24	26	24	26	24	26
25	29	25	29	25	27	25	27	25	27	25	27
26	30	26	30 May	26	28	26	28	26	28	26	28
27	31 Apr	27	1	27	29	27	29	27	29	27	29
28	1	28	2	28	30	28	30 Jul	28	30	28	30
29	2	29	3	29	31 Jun	29	1	29	31 Aug	29	31 Sep
30	3			30	1	30	2	30	1	30	1
31	4			31	2			31	2		

APPENDIX 1.

Details about the English Setters

Plate

1 SHOW CHAMPION ELSWOOD RENMARK BARONET (born 19/12/63) by Sh.Ch.Senglish Early Mist ex Renmark Melody, bred by Mary & Patrick Neave, owned by Mr & Mrs W. Foss, a Blue Belton. Won 12 challenge Certificates, sire of 5 show champions and two further C.C. winners.

2 SHOW CHAMPION SUNTOP ROYALBIRD (born 17/6/60) by Suntop Songbird ex Suntop Lady Rosa bred and owned by Miss M. Barnes, a link in the chain of great stud dogs bred by the Suntop Knls who have so influenced the breed over the last 15 yrs. Suntop Songbird sired 6 sh.ch's. Royalbird only at stud in this country for a short time after winning his 4th C.C. went to the U.S.A. where a short while afterwards he was poisoned. Sired three Sh.Ch's.

3 SHOW CHAMPION IROQUOIS STRATHSPEY (born 1/8/66) Orange/Belton. by sh.ch. Iroquois Stormcloud ex Sh.Ch. Iroquois Cascade. Bred and owned by Mrs. L. Allan-Scott. Very much a link pin in the great breeding line of Mrs. L. Allan-Scotts English Setters. Winner of 3 C.C.'s. Sire of Four Sh.Ch's.

4 WEST OF ENGLAND LADIES KENNEL ASSOCIATION 1966
Judge Mr C. Upton
Dog C.C. & B.O.B. 'Baronet'
Bitch Mrs A. Broadheads, Sh.Ch. Ernford Chaffinch who was out of Sh.Ch. Ernford Rosy Dawn who was out of Sh.Ch. Ernford Evening Flight — three of the most beautiful typical bitches seen. Chaffinch was the dam of the two Sh.Ch. brothers Ernford Falcon and Monksriding Ernford Flamingo. She later went to Canada and also became a Canadian Ch.

5 ENGLISH SETTER ASSOCIATION 1973
Judges Bitches Mrs V.C. Yates
        Dogs Mr N.J. Perkins
THE DOUBLE, owners of both Mr & Mrs H. Wheeler. Mr Wheeler handling Sh.Ch. Fenman Fragrance. Orange Belton. By Sh.Ch. Engsett Electrode ex Oldholbans Jay bred by Mrs E. Truman owned by Mr & Mrs H Wheeler. Winner of 7 C.C.'s. Mrs Wheeler handling Sh.Ch. Engsett Electrode. By Sh.Ch. Engsett Encounter ex Sheena of Frejendor Tri. B.I.S. National Gundog Ch. Show and Edinburgh Ch. Shows 1972. Sire of 4 Sh.Ch.'s winner of 7 C.C.'s.

6 LEICESTER CHAMPIONSHIP SHOW 1971
Judge — Mrs G. Wheeler
Mr. G.F. Williams Sh.Ch. Bournehouse Meadowfern by
Eveningflight of Frejendor (2 C.C.'s) ex Iroquois Jasmine bred
by owner winner of 3 C.C.'s dam of 1 Sh.Ch.
Mrs V. Foss's C.C. and B.O.B. then Best-in-Show Leicester 1971
Sh.Ch. Elswood Ashpenda Moonquest. By Sh.Ch. Elswood
Rnmark Baronet ex Sh.Ch. Iroquois Bluemoon bred by Mrs C.
Duffield. Winner of 6 C.C.'s.

7 ENGLISH SETTER ASSOCIATION 1970
Judge — Mrs P. Gardiner — Swann
C.C. and B.O.B. Mrs C. Ercolani's Sh.Ch. Yankee of
Neighbours by Shiplake Skidby's Guy Fawkes ex Silbury Satin
of Neighbours. Winner of 3 C.C.'s.
Mrs A.M. Tates Sh.Ch. Trodgers Meadow Fescue by Ch.
Boisdale Puffin ex Trodgers Red Clover. Winner of 7 C.C.'s.

8 Mr S. Boultons. Sh.Ch. EDNASID MERRELL BLUE
BARON. By Sh.Ch. Ednasid Wuster ex Gorsebrook Blonden
By Mrs A. Keneally winner of 9 C.C.'s.

9 Mr. H. Schofield's Sh.Ch. JEWEL OF THRUMALL. By
Mawdsley Thrumall Talent ex Mawdsley Bella By Mr T.W.
Watkinson Winner of 5 C.C.'s.

10 Mrs. A. Williams Sh.Ch. SILBURY SOAMES OF
MADAVALE By Silbury Sherper ex Silbury Springhead
Serene. bred by Mr & Mrs P. Gardiner-Swann. The greatest
winning English Setter to date winner of 24 C.C.'s Best-in-Show
Crufts 1964. Reserve Best in Show Crufts 1961 and 1963.

11 Mr & Mrs R. Goutorbes Ch. UPPERWOOD ZOE bred by Mr
Goutorbe by Sh.Ch. Engsett Electrode ex Withinlee winner of 9
C.C.'s and qualified in the Field.

12 Mr J & D & Mrs P Baldwins Sh.Ch. ELSWOOD WHITE
HEATHERETTE. Bred by Mrs F. Johnson by Sh.Ch. Elswood
Renmark Baronet ex Bousave Blue Elle. Winner of 3 C.C.s.

13 Mrs M. Marsden Sh.Ch. FENCEOOT FRECKLES by Sh.Ch.
Suntop Royal Sunglint ex Fencefoot Fatmiss Breeder owner
winner of 5 C.C.'s.

14 Mrs H. Parkinsons Sh.Ch. and American Sh.Ch. CLARIHO
WHIMSEY OF VALLEY RUN. Winner in this country of 9
C.C.'s plus gundog groups winner of her title in the U.S.A.
previous to being imported by Mrs. Parkinson.

Srvd Jul	Due to Whlp Sep	Srvd Aug	Due to Whlp Oct	Srvd Sep	Due to Whlp Nov	Srvd Oct	Due to Whlp Dec	Srvd Nov	Due to Whlp Jan	Srvd Dec	Due to Whlp Feb
1	2	1	3	1	3	1	3	1	3	1	2
2	3	2	4	2	4	2	4	2	4	2	3
3	4	3	5	3	5	3	5	3	5	3	4
4	5	4	6	4	6	4	6	4	6	4	5
5	6	5	7	5	7	5	7	5	7	5	6
6	7	6	8	6	8	6	8	6	8	6	7
7	8	7	9	7	9	7	9	7	9	7	8
8	9	8	10	8	10	8	10	8	10	8	9
9	10	9	11	9	11	9	11	9	11	9	10
10	11	10	12	10	12	10	12	10	12	10	11
11	12	11	13	11	13	11	13	11	13	11	12
12	13	12	14	12	14	12	14	12	14	12	13
13	14	13	15	13	15	13	15	13	15	13	14
14	15	14	16	14	16	14	16	14	16	14	15
15	16	15	17	15	17	15	17	15	17	15	16
16	17	16	18	16	18	16	18	16	18	16	17
17	18	17	19	17	19	17	19	17	19	17	18
18	19	18	20	18	20	18	20	18	20	18	19
19	20	19	21	19	21	19	21	19	21	19	20
20	21	20	22	20	22	20	22	20	22	20	21
21	22	21	23	21	23	21	23	21	23	21	22
22	23	22	24	22	24	22	24	22	24	22	23
23	24	23	25	23	25	23	25	23	25	23	24
24	25	24	26	24	26	24	26	24	26	24	25
25	26	25	27	25	27	25	27	25	27	25	26
26	27	26	28	26	28	26	28	26	28	26	27
27	28	27	29	27	29	27	29	27	29	27	28 Mar
28	29	28	30	28	30 Dec	28	30	28	30	28	1
29	30 Oct	29	31 Nov	29	1	29	31 Jan	29	31 Feb	29	2
30	1	30	1	30	2	30	1	30	1	30	3
31	2	31	2			31	2			31	4

ADDRESSES

The Kennel Club,
1 Clarges Street,
Piccadilly,
London. W1Y 8AB

The English Setter Association,
Secretary Mrs V Foss,
    Greenhill,
    Reservoir oad,
    Woolton,
    Liverpool L25 Telephone No: 051 428 5012

The English Setter Club (The Field Trial Side)
    Dr J Maurice,
    Batts Farm,
    Wilton,
    Marlborough,
    Wilts.

The Northern English Setter Society.
Secretary Mr. S. Crane,
    29, Woodside,
    Witton Park
    Bishop Auckland,
    Co. Durham.
    Telephone No. 0388 3630

The Setter & Pointer Club,
Secretary Mr G Coupe,
    Timadon Kennels,
    Woodside,
    Ashton,
    Nr Chester Telephone No: 08295 1505